Military Confessions Volume 1:

Raw & Uncut

"Adventures of SoldierSlim" By:

Wynston "A.P." Hightower

Cadmus Publishing
CadmusPublishing.com

A Wealthy Tortoise I.G. Production

Military Confessions Volume 1: Raw & Uncut
The Adventures of SoldierSlim

 Published by Cadmus Publishing LLC. P. O. Box 8664. Haledon, NJ 07538

Web: Cadmuspublishing.com
Business email: admin@cadmuspublishing.com

ISBN# 978-1-63751-542-6

Book Catalog Info Categories:
Urban fiction

Cadmus Publishing
CadmusPublishing.com

Introduction

Before we get into the intricacies of the stories to follow, I'd like you to think on the following questions and answer them, whether aloud or silently in your head, just so you can get a grasp the premise behind each story's tagline. What song, or songs, take you back to your first kiss; the first time you made love or had sex; had your first heartbreak; the first time you laughed, cried, or had a family reunion? These questions are important to the theme of **Military Confessions** as this series will explore some of these themes, thus allowing you to enter an intimate side of your servicemembers. We hope you'll enjoy this teaser into the upcoming series, and we look forward to sharing our stories.

The American military is comprised of some of the most elite and intelligent people in the world, but for some of us entering the military, especially at a young age, it's more akin to college. This includes lots of drinking, sex, and overall fun, at least until it's time to go to war, then it's all business. We've decided to let you in on some of our off-duty private military moments, and to protect people's identity and reputations, every person who contributed to this publication will hereby be known as "Soldier Slim".

We ask that you don't judge us by our most natural and animalistic pleasures as we were and still are the best at our occupation. Sex is as natural as the sun rising in the east and setting in the west, plus we know that some of our readers are just as sexual as we were. I caution you that some of these stories may make your toes curl and have you reminiscing on your own sexual encounters with the descriptions, so feel free to release your inhibitions while reading. And if any of you readers happen to recall any of these events as vividly as we did or willingly participated, then thank you for allowing your service members to perform their civil duties on your bodies and we hope you enjoyed those sexscapades as much as we did. Without further adieu, we'd like to welcome you to *Military Confessions Volume 1: Raw & Uncut.*

LORI

"I came fast like 9-1-1 in white neighborhoods; ain't got no shame *'bout* it. "J. Cole: *No Role Models*

Lori was in her early thirties when we met on Tango. She was Native American and had perfect features: buttery skin, nice C-cup breasts, and like that boy J. Cole said, *"she had a body that would make a gay nigga reconsider"'.* At the time I was going through a divorce: my wife and kids had left me three weeks ago, and it was my twenty-sixth birthday. I'd been off the market for nine years, but I was instantly drawn to her profile pic and the dress she was rocking, so I messaged her. We started kicking it back and forth, and she eventually told me to met her at her place of work later on in the week. From our conversations, I could tell she had the attitude of a grown woman. Her voice was sultry and seductive, like an old courtesan; I swear if I was into phone sex and she was an operator, I would've gone broke; however, I wasn't and things were about to change once she met Soldier Slim.

As a Black man, you should NEVER go half steppin' when you are about to slide, so that Friday I went and got the waves poppin' and met her after work. I considered going in my military uniform but decided to show up in civilian clothes. I wore black Levi boots, black 501*'s*, my black and gold Ralph Lauren custom polo, and my Georgia Tech snapback along with my Polo shades; to set it off I threw on some Ralph Lauren Double Black cologne. I was scheduled to met her at 8 p.m. when she got off, so I showed up around 7:30 p.m. It was still daylight in Alaska, so I had the Caddy truck polished and my 4's sitting pretty. I pulled up bumpin' Kevin Gates and Pusha T's song "Trust"; the windows were down and I was cruisin' through the parking lot.

Eventually I found a nice spot close to the store, so I parked and hopped out. Immediately upon exiting I start getting looks from other women; I don't mean to toot my own horn but I was a handsome Black man standing 6'5", looking good, smelling good, and riding clean, but barely noticed them as I had only one woman on my mind; as a Scorpio, I go hard when I'm really into a woman. While I slowly made my way inside, I text Lori to let her know I'd pulled up on her and then I proceed to ask her location. She immediately texts back a smiley face and messaged that she's upstairs in the eating area No cap, I was a little nervous, because as I said I'd been off the market for so long. Plus, I didn't want to be disappointed cause pictures can lie or get catfished because, and this was before FaceTime; however, when I entered the store and made my way to the eating area I wasn't prepared for what I saw as I ascended the stairs.

Lori was waiting with one of her female coworkers, an attractive white girl with a nerdy look similar to Nina Debrov in that Triple X movie. I slightly lost my cool when I laid eyes on Lori. She stood up to greet me and I whispered *,,Damn"* to myself. Lori was way more attractive than I'd anticipated. Even in her red work polo and khaki pants you knew she had it going on. She was a natural beauty and her face had the glow of freshly polished gold. Eventually I regained my composure and flashed my signature smile; fellas you know the one I'm talking about, not the shit-eating grin, but the devilish playboy smile that you master when you're young. Ladies you know it too, it's a mixture of the LL Cool J but we throw in a little lip bite similar to what we do when we are getting ready to kiss you and grab your ass at the same time. Anyhow, let's continue.

Shorty had a nose ring and one of those face studs that imitates a beauty mark. Upon further inspection, I noticed that her perfectly natural breasts were slightly erect and pierced; it didn't help that those work pants fit her frame exceptionally well, showcasing her generous childbearing hips and a superbly large "cameltoe." After I'd recovered from surveying this beautiful woman, I quickly introduced myself to the women then Lori and I embraced for a hug where I glanced at her backside and saw how it seemed to scream to jump out those pants while catching a hint of a black thong. I had to do everything in my power not to get a bulge in my jeans, especially after smelling her Dior perfume and seeing that she looked good enough to eat, which she eventually was, but let's not get too far ahead of ourselves.

We conversed for a while and eventually ended up back where she worked so that she could clock out. At the time she was working in the wine and spirits section of Fred Meyers, which was only a plus in my mind because I thoroughly enjoy my cognac and it was another reason to come see her, even though the PX was cheaper. At her scheduled time, she clocked out and we went outside to talk some more. She had a roommate she lived with and had to wait for the person to come pick her up, so we waited in my truck. Conversation was good and we settled on continuing to met up as we had some mutual attraction and chemistry. Plus, she liked my pretty brown eyes, big lips, and mischievous smile; that always gets 'em.

I'm a lover boy at heart, so I continued to show up to her place of business everyday I got off work for a **week** straight, because I was definitely into this woman. After some courtship, eventually things head into the realm of the physical. Our turn of events happened on a Saturday night after I'd hit the local club, had a few drinks, and contemplated hitting my Plan B. My other option was turning down for the night and playing *Call of Duty: Black Ops;* however, before I could decide, Lori texted me and asked me to come through and scoop her up. It was like 2a.m. in the morning and as my grandma told me, "Ain't nothin' open that late at night but legs", which I hope would be true. I hit her back and told her to give me like 30 minutes, only because I didn't want to seem too thirsty and it gave me an excuse to not head over.

After waiting the obligatory 30 minutes, I hit her back stating I'm on the way and asked where could we link. She hits me back and tells me the convenient store right off 24th Street. That was a skip and a hop for me, so I hit the autostart on the whip and let it warm up, then I head out into the cold Alaskan winter to see if I can hide my black Eskimo in her igloo. A short two minute drive later, I arrived at the appointed location and she walked over to meet me at the store. I was parked on the side of the place so she saw my truck and hopped in. We sat and talked for a while, and sipped a lil' sum sum. This went on for about 20 minutes and it felt right to make a move, so I casually kept the conversation flowing then slide my hand into her lap while pretending to grab the pint she had. She didn't react so I let me hand linger on her thigh as we continued to talk and listen to music. From there, we progressed into a little foreplay, some kissing, and light biting which leads into the good stuff.

We're grown, it's late, and we both know what time it is, so she tells me to pull around back. Nothing else needed to be said; I tum the ignition over, leave the lights off, and begin the journey around the back of the store. Mind you it's winter, I have rims, and the back of the store was a dirt road with lots of bumps and ruts, but who cares when you about to get balls deep into some fresh vagina. It was difficult trying to find a spot but I eventually settle on parking in the middle of this dirt path, facing the store just in case I had to haul ass. Once I did that I switched the music over to my R&B playlist to set the mood right.

I'm ready to go at this point, so my lady friend casually slid off her pants and instructed me to slide my seat back, but I couldn't go back any further because my tall ass already had it fully back. That didn't matter because we ended up making it work; I laid the seat down so that I was damn near laying in the middle row, and proceeded to pull my joint out. Lori crawls over into the driver seat, hops on top reverse cowgirl style and proceeds to inch her way down my shaft; my dick was so hard, I swear I could've made a metal detector go off. No lie, that was one of the best feelings in the world watching my manhood penetrate her beautiful mound, especially with her pussy being phat and extremely wet. She definitely had the most delightful box I'd ever seen; top three, no doubt. It was clean shaved, no bumps, and no odor; in the words of Plies, *"that pussy smelled like water"*. I eventually nicknamed her Starburst because she was unexplainably juicy.

She rode me slow and we got into a good rhythm that sounded like low waves shifting back and forth on the beach after sunset; it felt delightful piercing her exposed flesh, almost to the point of pure ecstasy, we were a perfect fit for each other. Things got so good that at one point I had to stop her because I would've came early like a Sunday morning church service at a Black church. When I pulled out, my pipe glistened like a naked body emerging from a cool swim in the take on a summer day: glowing, invigorated, and restless with energy. I had to go back in for another dip, and take advantage of the warm water.

I knew that if I started stroking again I'd lose the battle, so to even the odds I raised my seat up just enough to do a few things. After doing that, t slid back into the depths of this woman: however, this time to even the odds I had to do some sensory overload. This involved playing with the little man in the boat, which I found out was pierced as well, while she slid up and down on me excreting all her juicy goodness, as well as pulling her hair slightly and occasionally biting her neck and ear. I felt my own release coming soon, so I stop everything I was doing and grabbed her hips. I push her forward so that she's leaning into the steering wheel and pushed every inch into her; watching her throw it back as I hip thrust into her center. She continuously let out moans of pleasure as t slammed into her rhythmically.

My imminent release rapidly approached and she intermittently stated, *"Oh...Shit...I'm...Cummin"* My senses heighten at those powerful words and I shot the club up about five minutes later. She was upset, or at least pretended to be, because I sprayed her walls with no protection. I mean what did she think was gone happen since a nigga didn1have a rubber? t know I was a little reckless. but I chalk it up to my youth, and she had the birth control IUD or whatever it's called.

After we finished, she hops off and moved back into the passenger seat. I reached into the backseat and rumble around in my field bag, grab some baby wipes, and we clean ourselves up. FYI: I had baby wipes on deck because we occasionally went to the field and I kept my Army bag in my truck. As I cleaned myself, t couldn't believe how juicy that thing really was; the entire front of my pants were soaked to include my boxers, and I had juices flowing to my balls and ass crack. Now you see why I nicknamed her Starburst.

We continued to mess around daily. I'd show up to her job after work, and we had a no-strings-attached relationship. She just wanted me to be honest with her about if rm messing with another woman, and vice versa, which was exactly what I wanted at that point. This all worked out for a while until I didn't hold up my end of the deal, and I realized that she'd caught feelings after I brought Kassie to come stay the weekend at my apartment while Lori was there; things worked out with that situation as you'll see later. Long story short, Lori became my long-term lady until she passed four years later from anillness, but I did have other women I courted in our open relationship. For the most part she remained loyal and faithful to me, even though I'd let the old me out to play once again. I believe it worked out for us because she was a Pisces and I a Scorpio, which are highly compatible. I'll definitely fill you in on Kassie, but for now, let's move on to Part II of my encounter with Lori.

Lori Pt. 2

By this time we'd been messing around for about three months and Lori was **really** digging this young, handsome fella; she'd already dropped the "L" word on yaboy, but she said it was only because she misunderstood my text message when I told her "I love the things you do for me," to which she text back uI love you too" only to try and take it back when she realized what I truly said. During this point in our situationship she was helping me look for a place since I had been kicked out of on-post housing, plus she was doing little extra things to make a man feel good and comfortable; the things you'd expect from your wife type things.

I was staying with some associates of mine and paying $500 a month, but they were kind of ready for me to leave due to my dipping in and out the crib with various females, which was why Lori was helping me find a new setup; she didn't know about the others at this time. Anyhow, I wanted to show my appreciation for speaking my Love Language (acts of service), so I took two weeks of leave and paid for a week at a nice hotel in order to spend some QT (quality time) with what was essentially the wifey.

I spent around $800 for a week's stay at the hotel, but the memories created were well worth it now that I look back on it One of the greatest memories occurred on a Friday while staycationing with the lady. We spent the first half of the day chilling in bed doing the grown, cuddling, and talking about any- and everything. The afternoon was passed looking for a spot to rent, eating out, and restocking our alcohol for the night. After spending most of our day out on the town, we settled back at the hotel around 8 p.m. I recall walking to the elevator to head up to the room, drop off the things we purchased, change, and go to the pool. While waiting on the elevator, I got it in my mind that I'd never had sex in an elevator.

When the elevator arrived, it was empty, so we got in and I pushed up on the back wall while Lori stood in front of me. She pressed the number 10 to go to our floor; once the door closed it was on. I immediately grabbed her by the waist and pulled her towards me. It surprised her but she went with the flow of things. Her marshmallow soft ass we pressed against my rapidly hardening piece; I grabbed a hand full of her hair and pulled it slightly to the left so I could get access to her ear and neck, then I whispered u1 never had sex in an elevator and I want you to make it happen." I then proceed to nibble on her ear and slide my tongue down her neck as she released a moan like I was penetrating her soul. As I did this, she dropped the bags in her hands while I simultaneously placed my hand into the "coochiecutters" she was wearing; mind you she was the type to hardly wear underwear and like I told ya'll before, that cameltoe was swollen.

I'm working her up good, and we still haven't reached the top floor yet. She's hot and bothered now, so she turns around. I see that look in her eyes like "you better come handle yo business." I know what time it is, but I also know that we're really not gonna make it happen, so I have this shit-eating grin on my face because I know my little nympho is in the mood; however, she ain't letting me off the hook, so she proceeds to unbuckle my jeans and start to pull my shit out to return the favor. Before she can get that thang jumpin' the elevator stops on the 8th floor and standing there is a family with their children. Luckily the shotgun was loaded, but still in the safe, however, there was some embarrassment on her behalf. To cover up our illicit act, she simply turned around and pressed up on me while we rode the elevator the next two floors. To further add to this embarrassment, the couple gets off on the same floor and went in the opposite direction to their room all the while laughing about us almost being caught no doubt.

We break off to the right to go to our room, but we're walking slow and laughing at ourselves as well. It was fun and exciting almost getting caught with our pants down, literally. Our room was at the end of the hallway, so we had a ways to go before we ended up at our destination. While walking to our room, almost on top of each other like love-struck teenagers, we happened to hear a woman getting her back blown out; she wasn't being shy about it either.
She decides to stop in the middle of the hallway to listen for a peep, then she yells out *"Get that dick girl"* and we move on to our room.

Once we get inside, we drop off the bags and start to fool around a little. Things got hotter than a Southern Baptist's sermon on Easter with no air conditioning. She was still moist from the elevator situation and now my manhood was pressed up against my jeans like an infantry assault team preparing for a breach. So I grab Lori and guide her to the bed, then I straddle her, kiss her, and tell her how bad we wanted her. By now she's practically panting, wanting me to give her this country boy backwood. I knew this would have to be a quickie because I still wanted to hit the pool, so I proceed to kiss her more, then moved slowly down her body: first, her neck where I placed light kisses and sucked like I'm catching the juices of a tasty Georgia peach; next, I masterfully move to her big, beautiful golden breasts and place a small hickey in between both (she always disliked it afterwards); after that, I slid my hand underneath her shirt for a better view of my girls. Once I do, I licked her from the low cut of her shorts to her collar bone while removing her shirt as I go. Once the obstacle is removed, I proceed to roll my tongue and lips to my favorite place on earth.

She cried, *"Baby, please put it in already. I'm so damn horny right now."* I enjoyed every moment of it, but I held out. I continue on with my mission of pleasing and teasing her with foreplay. Now I'm at her waist line and I can practically smell the juices flowing from her sweet honeypot. I begin to slowly remove her shorts, which her pussy juice has already bled through, and what is revealed to me can only be described as a gift from God. It was nothing new to me, but it always made me grow that extra inch in my manhood. There was nothing but a clean shaven, round mound of slip-n-slide staring back at me; the wetness of it reminded me of being in a deep sleep and waking up because you've drooled so much that the whole side of your face and pillow is soaked--yeah, I'm talking that type of wet.

Pre-cum was leaking out of my joint at this point; he's ready to go like a Pitbull in mating season, however, it's still not the time to give her the grown man. Once her shorts are off, I stand up and remove my clothing; pants and underwear, then lastly my shirt. By the time I get my shirt off, she'd already grabbed my throbbing dick and starts going to town. I wanted to fight her off, but she wasn't having that, at least at the moment. (Pause)

I'm back now; had to take a minute to breath because I was starting to rock up reliving the moment. Well, I let her have her moment of dominance for about a minute or so, then I regain control. I assertively grab her hair, because likes it, and I remove my glistening penis from her mouth, then proceed to let her know that I appreciate what she was doing but Daddy's taking back the wheel. She looked like a woman possessed; full blown lust in her eyes and a sexual hunger I'd come to know oh so well; I've woke up many nights to either ablow job or her riding me simply to get off. It's coming to a point where I have to fuck her, but I still needed my fix.

I instruct her to slide back up on the bed, which she does without further prompting, and she lays down and spreads her legs so I have a full view of her womanhood. I know that I said I called her pussy Starburst, but tonight she was Skittles, because I was about to taste the rainbow. I love what I see, but let her know I needed her to flip over and get on all fours. I'm sure she was thinking I was about to take her to pound town, but like I said, I needed my fix. She gets on all fours and backs that thang up to the edge of the bed where I'm standing; she thought she was slick too because she tried to back it up right on my piece. Once she's in place, I grab her waist and let her think I'm about to lay the pipe game proper; I take one hand and rub the head again her labia minora (inner lips). I even slide a few inches in just so I can hear her moan and arch her back; she thought she was getting exactly what she wanted. I tease her with some short-stroking, then I press in my full length. They say the pussy's good when it sounds like macaroni and cheese being mixed, but Kraft ain't have shit on Lori. I was caught up in the moment and how good it felt that I forget I'm supposed to eat my snack before I break her back, so I pull out before I'm too far gone and proceed to get a taste of that sweet apple pie between her legs.

Her pussy had a glaze that looked sweeter than a Krispy Kreme donut as I looked at her swollen mound. She dripping like sap from tree, and I loved every minute of it. It feels amazing when a woman's body reacts to you that way. She's still on all four, so I drop to my knees and lick around her labia majora (outer lips) and it's the sweetest taste of a woman I've ever had and I haven't even touched the whole honeypot yet. Next, I kiss her swollen clitoris then suck on it; I lock my lips on it and slowly spell my name with my tongue: S-O-L-D-I-E-R-S-L-I-M, ensuring I emphasized each little dash in-between. She's trembling at this point and tries to drown me by throwing it back. I stop what I'm doing and go check myself out in the mirror. I looked worse than a snot-nosed kid eating a ice cream for the first time. I head back to the bed and give her that mischievous smile, then inform her that I didn't appreciate her trying to drown me even though I'm a good swimmer. At this point I'm standing directly behind her, my dick super hard, and I know it's time to finally give her what she wanted, but before I do I take time to nibble and kiss both cheeks, with one final lick from clit to asshole. At the time, all I could think of was Trey Songz "Dive In" single.

Now it's time for that action, I slid in my lady with no resistance and instantly felt at home; this was a place made specifically for me and mines. So I take the time to flex in it, making it jump inside her walls; she returns the favor by flexing her vaginal walls right along with me, then she slowly starts to throw it back on me. It was hypnotizing watch her phat pussy grip my manhood, sliding back and forward on some grown woman shit. I'm deep off in the game now. It started out slow, with her looking over her left shoulder, moaning, and biting her lips; our rhythm sounding like a big dog lapping its bowl, then it got a little too good. Juices are running down my balls and I felt like I'd been caught in a torrential downpour; the way her pussy sounded was akin to running in rain storm on a quiet street while trying to avoid getting wet; all you hear is the splashing of footsteps.

I'm at the point I'm ready to release my seed deep into the heart of her warm center, but I feel owed an excitable moment. I get it in my mind that we should have sex in the middle of the hallway, so I withdraw my manhood and ask her to follow me. She rolls over and ask me in an aching yet frustrated voice *"where we're going?"*, to which I reply *"just follow* me *woman and you'll see."* I head towards the door with my erection leading the way; she's starting to catch on as I reach for the door and open it. Lori reached for something to cover up because she was afraid someone would walk by to see her, even though we're at the end of the hall. Her mouth is agape at my boldness of standing in the doorway stark naked and proceeds to ask me what I'm doing. All I say is *"bring yo ass on woman."*

Lori dropped her protective clothing, walked over, then stood between me and the door trying to close it, so I let her; I see this will take some convincing. She's standing there in all her God given beauty, still wet and horny, so I lean down and kiss her. She's very responsive to my lips, so I reach around and place my hands firmly on her ass and squeeze both cheeks as I continue to partake in a tongue wrestling match; I even manage to slide my middle finger into her slot to add more stimulation, prompting her to stand on her tippy toes. She moans and pants as we continue to lock lips; I'm about afoot taller than her, so I'm bent over while all this is happening. I move from kissing her lips down to her exposed neck area and continue to tickle her insides. Her eyes roll, she bites her lips, and her pussy tightens; she's ready to release one so I remove my finger before she finishes and tell her that if she wants relief then she's gonna have to follow me outside.

She whines, *"But baby I wanna finish right here in the room. I'm so close."* I get visibly upset and it shows on my face for like a microsecond, then I give her a devilish smile. I decided to oblige the lady and I lift her right leg and place it on my hip. Without further provoking, she wraps her arms around my neck and places the other leg on my other hip, and reaches down to introduce my mini me to her southern comfort. She starts to grind on me as our sex kiss passionately. Lori gets deep into it, working herself back to the point of climax; I feel her walls grip my hardened shaft, her eyes are closed--she's focused on her release--and that's when I make my move.

I take a step back, open the door while my right arm supports her, hold the door with my right foot and turn the lock switch; this will help to keep the door ajar in case we needed to step back inside. I look outside to see if the coast is clear and she starts to slow down, but I tell her that if she wants to cum tonight she better keep going. She calls me a *"dirty motherfucker"* and I smartly reply *"Yep, you're the only dirty mother I'm fucking."* She smiles and bites my neck, but continues to grind away. The coast is clear so we step into the hall with Lori still straddling me. I let the door close, but it's still ajar because of the lock. Once outside, I instruct Lori to stop and hop off real quick. Next, I move to the floor to where my head is facing the far wall and I can see down the hallway. At this point we're two naked people in the hallway; I'm laying on the floor with a rock hard erection that's standing at attention and a slight lean to the right, and she's standing there looking down at me.

Now that I'm in the position I want to be in, I have Lori climb on top of me and we continue what we were doing back in the room. I can tell she's nervous and kind of excited because she started looking around but had one of those mischievous smiles like when you do something you're not supposed to, but you do it anyhow because you think it's fun. My baby looks amazing in her birthday suit as she rode me cowgirl style in the middle of this hallway; her juicy breasts cupped in my hand, the swaying of her hips as she gyrates on my stick, and the way she was pressing down in my chest is a memory I'll always cherish. It didn't take long for us to reach our breaking point. I believe the mixture of fun, excitement, and possibly fear aided in us catching our nut.

Luckily for us, we weren't caught or at least didn't go to jail that night. Plus, we still made it to the pool in time to enjoy the Jacuzzi and swim a few laps after taking a shower. I was young and immature at the time, but we had some good times together before she passed. Plus, I'd grown to have deep feeling for her in our short time together. I joke and say I never want to get married again, but if I had the chance, she definitely would've been wife number two. Not just because of the sexual chemistry we had, but because of the level of maturity, the respect she had for me, and she possessed qualities in a grown woman that I now look for when I do decide to take someone as my other half. I can honestly say that Lori was the first woman I've loved; not some little girl pretending to be a woman or some crush, but a full grown ass woman. I miss you babe, and you're forever in my heart.

Kassie

I bet you love me more after the first fuck. I bet you love me more after you hear worse love. ...Imma make it mines, mines for the night, got me pulling on your hair."
-6lack ft. Jhene Aiko; *First Fuck*-

Kassie was introduced back in the story of Lori. She's mentioned here because earlier I mentioned that I'd NEVER relieved myself by fellatio, well Kassie was the first to almost do it and her mouth game was proper. Anyhow, this is a two part story: the first is how we met and later became sexually involved, the second is how her and Lori first met.

By now I'd been newly single, separated, or whatever you want to call it for a month. It was close to the holidays I enjoy the most: Thanksgiving and Christmas, but with no family around I decided to find other comforts. It was still exceptionally warm for the winter months in Alaska, so I decided to go out. My outfit for the night would consist of a salmon colored Ralph Lauren Polo shirt with the kiwi green horse, Ralph Lauren khaki's, black Ralph Lauren socks, and the Ralph Lauren shoes to match the shirt; something simple, but still fashionable. The whip was already clean, and all I required to complete the look was a fresh cut.

I jumped in the shower, cleaned myself up, and popped out to the barbershop before the nights festivities. I wasn't looking to get fancy or anything so I threw on my navy blue Dickie shorts; a black on black Atlanta Braves snapback; a black tee with the Masonic emblem on it with gold trim; crew cut Polo socks; and some black and yellow retro Jordan 1's, and dipped off to the shop. It was a non-payday weekend so it wasn't that packed, but I did have to wait behind three people. I greet my barber Aaron and he hollered back, *"What's up Polo?"*, because I wore so much of it and so did all six of the kids when we were together. When my tum came, we made conversation as he laced me up. I got it all: a temp- fade, facial, and razor line: my shit was like a Chinese buffet special-- extra crispy with duck sauce. Aaron always did me proper so I paid and left a $20 tip. He had the waves hitting harder than a fight between Mike Tyson and Kimbo Slice, so I captured it and posted to my Facebook page.

Once I posted my pie, I headed on post. My goal was to grab two bottles of Henny, some Ocean Spray CranGrape, Newports, and a pizza then head back to the crib and pregame until it was time to hit; however, I made a pit stop at the post gym to see if anyone was playing ball. It was a Saturday, so people Were usually in the gym and I always had some gear in the back. It turned out that people were there, even Carmen, which led to me playing ball for about two hours before everyone broke away for lunch. After that I completed my mission, went back to the crib, showered, and pregamed for the next few hours while alternating between playing different versions of *Call of Duty*, *Grand Theft Auto*, and *Need for Speed Dub Edition*.

At the time I was living with two roommates while looking for a place of my own; this is important because it led to me getting my own place, which carries over into part two of this story.

Well, it was late and I'd achieved a good buzz so I parlay on my drinking, and throw on my get-up. The time was about 11 o'clock and shit didn't really hit 'til midnight, so I sat around in a white beater, my Polo Khakis, and Polo loafers smoking a Newport 100 while channel surfing. I do this for the next 45 minutes or so, then I hit the autostart on my truck to get the juices flowing. While I wait for my vehicle to prime, I finish dressing myself. I throw on my shirt, chain, and hit myself three times with *Joop* cologne. Usually it would be Polo everything, and I had various Ralph Lauren cologne, but I wanted something different that night. Once set, I head out the door and made my way to the club.

I arrived on the scene about 12:15 or so, found some prime parking off to the side of the building, and made my way inside. Like I said before, it wasn't a payday weekend so most of the young enlisted weren't out that night unless their money was on point; however, the place was still full. Once inside, I made my way upstairs to the Hip-Hop section. The crowd was pretty decent so I found a table near the back and had the server bring me a brew and a Henny on the rocks. My plans for the night were simply get out the house and feel the vibes. I wasn't looking to take nothing down that night because I already had something for later on, but when you're out you never know what'll happen.

I stuck around until about 2 a.m. and was ready to wind down, so I make my way towards the exit but this woman caught my eye. She stood at the bar waiting to order something to drink. What caught my eye was the fact that she had a nice backside for a woman of her size; she's what we call slim thick. This woman was about 5'7", wearing some blue jeans that hugged her curves, a low-cut black shirt, and her hair was pressed and shoulder length; her skin was golden brown, slightly darker than whiskey, and she wore glasses, which gave her that sexy nerd vibe. I made a detour towards the bar and asked her what she was drinking and it turned out she was a vodka girl, so I ordered a shot for her and a Henny shot for myself; I was looking to make conversation but she quickly downed her shot before I got mines, so I bought her another one and quickly went to work before she could take off. I held her attention for about two minutes whereby I learned her name and got her number. Mind you, I'm not usually a straight forward type of guy, but I was digging this young lady, so I got to the point because I could tell she had other plans for the night and so did I.

No lie, I thought she'd played me because she gave me her nickname and I had no intentions of dialing her up right then and there to see if the contact was real. Things turned out great because she went and dropped the drinks off to her friends and came back to the bar where I was standing. We conversed some more and I even got a dance. Well, it was more like I stood there and she gyrated her ass against my manhood. I could tell she was a little freak because she kept looking back smiling and biting her lips. After the dance I got to know that she was from Anchorage and down here visiting some friends. This lasted for about 20 minutes, we made plans to catch up, and she returned to her friends while I finished off my second drink: a double Hen and a splash of cranberry.

I finished my drink and departed. Like I said before, it was exceptionally warm for the winter months, so I casually strolled to my vehicle. There was still about an hour or so left until the club closed and for some reason people were still pulling up. As I walked to my truck a caravan of cute white girls pulled up. One chick on the passenger side was very bold and rolled down the window of the Tahoe they were in and tried to holler at me. She told me she liked my outfit, and she hoped I wasn't leaving because she wanted a dance. I kept walking and played her off; being a young Black man from the country, I was told by my biracial grandmother to stay away from white women and it stuck with me until a few years ago. Now, if that happened today I'd have to slay her cute ass, but I digress. Anyhow, they parked and exited their vehicle. The woman that spoke to me had on some black spandex pants, a green crop-top, pink undershirt or sports bra, and some flats; she was cute as hell and had a nice little turd cutter on her, but I hopped in my whip and left regardless.

I went home and hit up Lori after leaving the club, and we have a nightcap at her little spot Throughout the week I text and converse with Kassie moving things in the right direction. We get to the point by the middle of the week where she scheduled a flight to come see me, on her own dime. I was excited because I'd just gotten out of a long-term relationship of 8 years and I'd been on the market only about a month, and here I was juggling six women. Don't get me wrong, some of them knew about each other and didn't care, and four of them knew my situation, so it wasn't like I was playing them or their emotions. We were all just having a good time.

It was a late Friday night when Kassie touched down in Fairbanks, Alaska and I picked her up in my new car. I'd crashed and totaled my truck earlier in the week after driving home from work; I made a left turn and started sliding on the ice and hit a fire hydrant. Now I was riding in a 2008 Chevy Impala. After picking Kassie up, I took her back to the place I was staying. Mind you I was staying with two roommates at the time. Once I got her back to the crib I took her bags inside and let her get comfortable by turning on the television, putting away the bags, and then sitting on the couch and let her put her feet up on my lap.

I don't pay attention to what's on TV because we mainly talked. She informed me that she was glad to be there and she'd been thinking about me all week. This woman was laying it on thick, so I played along. I let her know I felt the same and that I'd thought about her all week too. We did the normal things like talk about our week, how we were ready for this weekend, and how we'd been talking nasty to each other. It didn't take long for the temperature to rise, and soon she was asking where the bathroom was. I let her know it was upstairs and she grabbed her bag and dipped out for a few. After she cleaned up, she came back down and put away her bag, then proceeded to remove her pants right there in the middle of the living room.

She looked good in the ambient light of the television. I could see the contours of her backside and the cuppage on the bottom; I told you she had a little phatty for a semi-petite woman. And what set it off was the peach colored lace panties she had on. Kassie knew I was looking so she turned around with her little B-cup breasts and asked me did I like what I was looking at, to which I only grinned like a hungry wolf and said *"maybe."* With that she said, *"Maybe I need to come closer and give you* a *better look because it's dark and you kinda blind'*, so she slowly made her way towards me doing a sensual walk; come to find out, this woman was a skilled seductress, but I didn't learn that until months later.

Once she'd reached me, she turned around and asked me the same question as before, and I told her that it was a little better but I couldn't tell because her clothing was blocking my view. I think she enjoyed the fourplay, because she wiggled her ass then slowly removed her panties. She did it while playing coy on some Marilyn Monroe type shit, because when she got to the bottom of her cheeks she bent over and straight legged then continued taking off her underwear; I saw nothing but ass and a clean shaven twat. It was an intoxicating sight to behold. Once she'd removed her panties, she stood up and removed her bra. By this point, I'm hard enough to punch a hole in an IOTV. Once she was in her birthday suit, she had me stand up so she could lie on the couch. My erection screamed to burst out of my ESPN PJ's, and Kassie took notice, so she beaconed me over and removed it through the opening.

She sat up, placed me in her mouth, and held me there, gripping the tip of my penis tightly in her mouth while rolling her tongue in a circle over it. I looked down at her and she looked like one of those photos where the chick is doing the duck lips for her pics, so I smiled at her. At this prompting, she popped me outta her mouth while holding the base of my manhood, and asked me if I liked it. I let her know it felt good, but I'd never caught one off some head. She must've took this as a personal challenge because she laid back on the sofa, instructed me to remove all my clothing, then had me straddle her face over the sofa. Basically, I was planking on the sofa with my hands on the armrest and my hard on in her face.

She grabbed me with one hand and starts toying with the tip, while flicking her clit with her other hand. I had to give it to her, she had talent because she worked me and herself into a frenzy; I can't tap my head and rub my stomach simultaneously, and here she was sucking and jerking me off while playing with her pussy. I didn't blow my load in the time span she topped me off, and she was actually surprised because others had already popped their tops by now; the good thing was my shit was on super swollen like when Bruce Banner transforms into The Incredible Hulk. In a way I think not coming turned her on because she was like *"since my head game couldn't get you off, I bet this pussy will."* then she slid down on the sofa and spread her legs inthe missionary position with one cocked up over the back, so I maneuvered myself into position.

I'm leaning over her with my dick hovering around the entrance of her pussy, so I grab myself and tease her by rubbing the head between her folds. She' already wet, but never like Lori. On a side note, Megan thee Stallion was correct when she said that a woman ain't doing it right if you don't have to change the sheets, and there were many a times Lori and I changed our sheets and placed a towel in the wet spot, depending on whose side of the bed we fucked on.
Anyhow, when I saw Kassie's eyes get glossy I pushed myself inside her, not forcefully though. First, the tip pierced her and she gasps; she's tight but not too tight, like it's been a while since she's been penetrated, because her walls loosened their grip once I start digging deeper. Next, I push about half my length in, about four inches, and held steady right there rocking back and forth to climatize her to this heat. Finally, once I felt her body relax I push myself all the way in and watched as her eyes slightly bulge and her pussy tighten around my shaft.

Now I'm inside her all the way and I slowly start working her like a 9 to 5. I do that for about five minutes until she'd lathered me up all the way with her juices. Once that happens, I stuffed her like a Thanksgiving turkey, as she's enjoyed herself. She moaned like a cat in heat, and I had to tell her to keep quiet because I had roommates upstairs. She had me stop and grab her travel pillow. With that taken care of, I slid back between her legs once more and back in her guts. however, this time I pushed her left leg up so that I could really get up in there and hit those hard to reach spots. A young man like me was feeling good at this point because this was the second woman, who was older than me, who I was dicking down and doing a great job from her bodily reaction.

While I was doing my thang, Kassie seriously forgot my previous statement of having roommates and tossed the pillow so she could grab ahold of my ass and push me deeper in her wet walls. I now had a woman moaning, lost in the throes of passion, and occasionally biting my chest. That shit turned me on and I started trying to punish her. At this point I didn't care about my roommates, and a few moments later I shot my hot load inside her hole. She knew I'd cum because I made the "ugly face" and my seed spilled out of her, but that didn't stop our fuck fest This woman was prepared because she got up, went to her bag, grabbed some feminine wipes, cleaned herself up real good, and came back for seconds.

By this time I'm sitting upright on the sofa with a semi. Kassie looked at me and said,"*I hope you don't think we're done mister'*, then walks over to where I'm sitting and forced my legs outward so I'm sitting like most men when they're taking up space, then she squats right in front of me taking my little man in her hand. She starts playing with it and talking to it like, *"You did a good job, but mama needs more. Can you handle that?"* I told her I need a few minutes to get myself together but she tells me to shut up because this conversation doesn't involve me, it's between her and junior, so I shut the hell up and let this woman do her. She does a great job of coaxing my shit back to full hardness where she alternated between talking, jerking, kissing, and sucking on my genitalia. Once I reach maximum capacity, she casually stood up and boldly proclaimed, "*I told you that this didn't involve you, but the next part does"* and then straddled me over the sofa.

There's nothing but a clean shaven pussy staring at me eye level, because she's standing over me on the sofa. Next thing I know she starts dancing to whatever song was in her head, something similar to Selma Hayak in the movie *Dusk Til Dawn*. She even turned around and danced so I saw her phat little booty and pretty pussy hypnotizing me through her seductive movements. Once the "song" was over, she looked back at me and asked if I liked the show. I admitted I did and exclaimed the "we" were still ready for round two. She looked down and seen
that her "buddy" was still excited and smiled a smile that seemed to rival my own devilish grin.

Kassie stepped down off the couch, grabbed my hand, and walked me over to the recliner in the comer. She sat me down,dropped to her knees and starts bobbin'. She could've been a professional head doctor the way she gave me the business. I mean the way she slurped, popped at the head, and worked her hands were amazing. She even deep throated without shedding a tear, complaining, or gagging; however, she still didn't pop my head cherry. Once she saw I wasn't gonna coat her throat, she stopped sucking and only massaged it with her hands then straight up asked me with a challenging look in her eyes, *"so you really not gone cum in my mouth, huh?"* I had to let her know that it wasn't intentional and that her head was the best I'd had until now.

She took it in stride and was vocal about tasting me on way or another. Next thing I know she stood up, turned around, reached between her legs to grab my piece, then slid down my pole. She rode me reverse cowgirl style while using my knees as support. Imagine watching a fine ass woman grooving on the dance floor and you wonder to yourself, *"Can she doit witha dick in her?"*, well Kassie definitely could. While my dick made her pussy talk, I was about to reach nut number two. My body started tensing; I tried taking control so I could thrust harder in her, but was held in place by the recliner and her movements. I was ready to release my juice inside her once more and watch her cup overflow, but she had other plans. Kassie started to put it on me bad. I'm talking bout I wanted to scream like a little girl the way she was putting that pussy on me but I held my own. She must've felt my muscle start to spasm because on her upstroke she removed herself from my hardness, turned around, dropped to her knees, and started catching everything in her welcoming mouth. I felt I was releasing everything in me when she did that; it felt akin to Goku releasing a Spirit Bomb.

Once she finished her meal, we knew it was time to clean ourselves up, which meant shower time. She grabbed her peach laced panties and put them back on along with the yellow long tee I'd worn earlier, while I slipped back on my pajamas. Kassie stayed downstairs while I went upstairs to take a piss and start the shower, however, I was interrupted by my roommates.
They wanted to talk to me after I finished using the bathroom, so I do my business and come back out to talk. The conversation was about me bringing women in and out late at night and them making all that noise, it caused them not to sleep and was inconsiderate. I told them I paid half the rent, so it shouldn't matter who I brought in and at what time, but I promised to keep the noise down. Somehow it turned into an argument and Kassie came upstairs. She came to apologize for making noise and intruding on their sleep. We eventually smoothed things out, and I told Kassie to hit the shower while I talked to the woman of the house. The conversation was short, they wanted me out in 30 days and I said cool. After that, I hit the shower with

Kassie and made plans to find a place within the allotted time and cop a hotel for the weekend.

Saturday morning we left the crib and booked a hotel room for the next two days. Check-in wasn't until two so we stayed out grabbing things for ourselves, i.e. alcohol and smokes. At check-in time we headed back to my place to grab her things along with a few items for the weekend, and then we sped back to the room. We arrived at the hotel, took our things out, and settled down. The room was nice and it had two beds: one to sleep on and the other to.... you know the rest. I'd brought my laptop and external hard drive because I thought I'd be able to connect the HDMI cord and watch the thousands of movies I had on there, but the TV didn't allow for that, so we just watched basic cable television. Kassie placed the telly on Cartoon Network and I think Ed, Edd, and Eddy was on. We sat on separate beds, watched the show, and poured up some drinks. We spent time getting to know each other a little bit more and I learned that she was a private escort; I guess that explains her ability to lay it on thick and certain skills she had. She also told me that the services I'd 'gotten men paid her for and that she'd never paid her own money to come see a man before, so I should be grateful she liked me. I don't know if that was ego stroking or what not, but I got the big head in more ways than one.

I was ready to show her how grateful I was, so I placed my drink on the night stand, got off the bed and made my way to her. She must have known what I had planned because she had a sly smile on her face. Her head was slightly down so that she looked over her glasses and she asked me in the sweetest voice. *"What do you think you're doing, mister?"* I took that as a signal that I was going to have to work for it, so I stated with some sexual overtures that I came over to see what her drink tasted like because it looked so good. I told her I wanted some and proceeded to reach my hand out for her glass; I expected her to hand it over so I could make my move, but that didn't happen, at least not immediately. She looked up at my quizzically and asked me, *"Why share my drink with you when you didn't share yours?"* I told her that all she had to do was ask and I'd willingly share anything of mines she wanted, so she took me up on it and asked to partake in my drink. At this point I was going with the flow, because the vibes was feeling right so I asked her did she really want a sip of what's in my cup and was she serious. So I drunk the little I had left, then told her if she wanted to taste my drink she'd have to go through me.

She cheesed hard at my antics. At my prodding, she stood up, downed her drink, and repeated my exact words; I guess two could play this game. I liked the challenge so I leaned in and pecked her on the lips, then stood erect and told her that she tasted sweet but there wasn't any drink left, just residue. Next thing I know she closed the short distance between us, reached up, grabbed me by the nape of my neck, and planted a passionate kiss on me. I succumb to her feminine wiles and we tongue wrestled. We felt as one in the moment, so I brought her closer and reached down to squeeze and cup her soft backside, and like something out of a movie, she jumped and wrapped her legs around my waist. It was a good thing she weighed about a 130 pounds.

I held her while standing near the edge of the bed; I tasted a hint of the Ciroc and Sprite she'd been drinking mixed with the Henessey and cranberry juice I had. Our mouths and the aftermath of our alcohol made for a good mix, and I was aching for our bodies to do the same, so I turned towards the bed she was originally on, which was the one closest to the door, and I moved us to the bed. Kassie was underneath me and still going strong kissing and holding me in a leg wrap; by now I'm full erect, and since we were in the missionary position I lowered myself between her legs and grinded my erection against her in a counter clockwise manner. I stopped kissing her at that moment and let her know that she'd started something that I hoped she was ready to finish. She answered coyly, "*I don't know what you're talking about. You started with me first.*" From that answer I figured that this little game of cat and mouse was still on, so I continued to oblige.

From that point on I took control of the game and put the full court press on her. I told her to wait because it was getting too hot, then I stood up and took everything off except my gray boxer shorts. I did that just so she could see my erection and amp up the sexual energy in the room; I was so hard at this point that I was aching to break through my underwear like Jack Nicholson broke through the door in *The Shining*. Kassie was on the bed with her knees up, so I spread them apart, hooked my arms under her legs, pulled her to the edge of the bed, and gyrated my erection against her; at one point I pulled it out and slapped it against her print. I knew she was getting hot and bothered at this point, so I released her legs and let them touch the floor, then I took both her arms and placed them above her head and insisted that she not move.

I straddled her body placing my hands on the side of her hands with my legs across her lower body; mind you I still had my erection out in full view. I begin kissing the inside of her left wrist, occasionally nibbling and sucking as I made my way down her arm. I get as far as her elbow before I was hindered by the shirt she wore, but I don't let that stop me. I simply moved to the right arm and repeated the process until I reached her sleeve, then I moved to her neck, inhaled her perfume and told her that she smelled good enough to eat (for the record, no I didn't go down on this one). I then bit her softly, which earned me a moan of pleasure and the slight arching of her back; I had to remind her that I told her not to move, so I whispered in her ear that if she did it again I'd have to hold her down. She promised to be a good girl and I continued to pursue the end goal of us both being pleasured.

Her collarbone was exposed, so I kissed her center, to the right side, all the way to the left. I licked, kissed and sucked my way up her neck until I reached her ear, at which point I nibbled from her earlobe to the top of the ear, then traced my way back down with my tongue. Next, I kissed from her ear to the top of her forehead and moved to the left side until I reached her other ear. From there I licked around that ear from top to bottom and once I reach Kassie's earlobe I bite her slightly harder because I wanted her to move, and she did. I immediately grabbed both her hands with my left hand and let her know that she'd disobeyed a direct order and asked her what her punishment should be. She exclaimed that I cheated and that I wasn't playing fair. I had to let her know that if you ain't cheatin', you ain't tryin', at least that's what I was taught in the Army. I asked her again what her punishment should be, and she told me I can decide. I figured this was a test to see if I would go ahead and fuck or extend the foreplay; I wasn't new to this so I extended the foreplay. I released her and told her to take off her shirt while I set up.

I grabbed my computer and speakers and setup some music. While Kassie removed her shirt, I placed the speaker and computer on the dresser and opened my iTunes account. Once inside the app, I located my R&B folder that I created for my iPod, then scrolled through to find the most suggestive song I had in mind. What I didn't know was that she'd removed more than her shirt, she'd also removed her pants. I found the song I wanted, which was *Headboard* by Mario, but before I could press play Kassie chose that moment to move behind me, wrap her arms around me and with her right hand she started to massage my hard-on. I smiled and hit play. I let her do this until the chorus hits: "*I put you up against the headboard, gettin' all wild, fuckin' like we tryna have a child...*", then I grabbed and gently removed her hand, then turned around and saw her in a matching red lace panty and bra set. Red was never my color but in that moment it was my favorite; I still have the picture saved in my email account.

I gave her the most beautiful smile I could muster and if she was a few shades lighter, she would have blushed. At that moment I lifted her hand in the air, and at my prompting she does a slow turn; I take in her beautiful curves: her ample bottom, the curve of her back and width of her small hips, and the way her breasts rested inside her bra. Once her showcase was complete and we were face to face again I pulled her close, grabbed her by the waist, then leaned down and whispered in her ear, *"You're definitely one of the most beautiful women I've had the pleasure of pleasing, and I know what your punishment will be for disobeying me."* After I said my peace, I bit her ear, grabbed both her cheeks, then gave each one a playful slap.

The music played from my selected playlist while all of this is going on, but I wasn't quite ready to administer punishment yet, so I once again take her hand into mine and we walk over towards the sink where the mirror was. I had her stand in front of it, while I stood behind her. She smiled at me and asked, " *What are you doing?",* to which I tell her" *Let me do me and enjoy the moment."* I began removing her bra freeing her golden brown beauties and tic-tac sized nipple; once I do, they sat on her chest fully erect. By this point she's looking down like she was bashful, which I later found out she some insecurities along with other problems, but in that moment I wasn't fully aware of it. Anyhow, I noticed her, so I placed my hand underneath her chin and lifted her face so that she was looking directly into the mirror with me looking directly back at her through our reflection.

I informed Kassie that she had nothing to be ashamed of and that in this moment she was the single, most perfect woman in the world and I wouldn't trade her places with any other woman, no matter who or how famous they were. She moved like she wanted to turn and face me, but I don't let her, so she simply leaned back and asked me was I serious, to which I said *"most definitely."* I see tears form in her eyes and she tells me I'd treated her better in the week we've known each other than all the men in her life, including the father of her son; she also told me that she felt like a woman with me instead of just apiece of ass, and she felt the lucky one. It must have been destined, because once she finished that statement one of my favorite songs by the group TGT came on, which was *Sex Ain't Never Felt Better.* I chose that moment to kiss the top of her head and let her know that I was the lucky one because she chose me to share her body with; she definitely could have any man she want but she chose me and I was about to show her why she made the right choice.

She looked up at me and I leaned down to kissed her. Usually when people are kissing in that manner, your eyes and you become consumed by the moment, but I kept mines open because I wanted to see her facial expressions. I then placed my right hand on her stomach and made my way to her crotch through the top of her panties; she invitingly let me in. My hand found that she was very saucy, so I slipped my middle and ring finger into her center and continuously penetrated her; she emitted a rolling moan as I do so and started to move in sync with my rhythm. With my left hand now free, I took the opportunity to cup her left breast in my long and dexterous fingers and began to rotate my thumb and pointer finger around the nipple.

At that particular moment she opened her eyes and saw my eyes open and she playfully bit my lip. I stopped everything I was doing so that she could turn around and face me, then I pressed her into the counter and proceeded to express more of my feeling towards her. I let Kassie know that I appreciated her sharing her body with me and that I felt privileged because our bodies are precious and engaging in sexual relations is like an ultimate form of trust. She asked why was that, and I told her that people are at their most vulnerable in that state. Two people are naked, sharing their sexual energy and bodies with each other, while trusting that neither will do anything to violate or cause harm to the other. Essentially you've allowed another person to enter your space, and for a woman that has double meaning. As I said that I grabbed her legs and slid her on the counter of the sink and stood in between those gorgeous thighs.
Kassie then said, *"You know all the right things to tell a woman to get what you want, huh?"* I looked down at her pretty little pussy pressing through her panties, bite my lower lip, and stated, *"If what I say is the truth, I can't help how that makes you feel sweetheart."*

The vibes were heightened at this point. It was like being a young teenager on a date and you know the girl likes and wants you, but you don't want to rush to the kissing part or blow it; you feel the energy between the two of you, your body is tingling and senses are in overdrive because of the flood of endorphins. Well, that was what it felt like in that moment with Kassie, so I just smiled, leaned in, and kissed her on the lips. Nothing serious, just a sensual peck. For some reason, at that moment, the O'Jays song *"Cry'* cycled through the playlist. I couldn't help but laugh; you know, one of those laughs where you feel it in your lower abdomen but the air is released through your nose. I felt like a man possessed as I let my alter ego take over. Even though a love song was playing, I knew that making love wasn't in the books for either one of us; the only things that were going down was her on me, some good fucking, and maybe my erection after I was done.

I took Kassie's hand and said, *"Let's go back into the bedroom."* She hopped down, grabbed my hand, and led the way. When we got to the bed she turned around to try and kiss me, but I didn't allow her. I let her know that play time was over and I still owed her from earlier, so I instruct her on what she needed to do. I told Kassie to turn around and stand at the foot of the bed; while she did I switched the song to Lil Boosie's *Distant Lover*. After I completed that I walked up behind her, reached around her body and cupped both nipples while pinching them. Next, I whispered in her, *"I'm gone fuck you real good tonight. You probably gone fall in love with a nigga."* I was feeling myself and definitely on my Scorpio shit yet again.

Once I whispered those words, I stepped back, and removed my gray boxer briefs, then placed myself closer to her. I told her to follow my lead and I took my right hand and placed it in the middle of her back to guide her forward, then I took my left and placed it on the back of her left hamstring. My next words to her were, " *Keep your hands on the bed. Once you do, you will slide up just enough so that you can put this leg, the one I'm touching with my left hand, upon the bed; once you do, put anarch in your back and don't move."* Kassie did as instructed and I had a nice view of her wet pussy through her red lace panties. The song I put on is still playing in the background, so I take my left hand and pull her panties to the side and hook it with my thumb. I then take my right hand and start digitally penetrating her one finger at a time; first my pointer finger, then my middle finger, and finally my ring finger. Those fingers are working her and stirring her juices, and it's turning both of us on. My dick felt angrier than Wolverine in a berserker rage.

I removed my ring finger from her now soaked pussy and massaged her clit with my thumb. This goes on for a while before I give in, and decided it was time to give her some wood. I had her place her other leg up on the bed before I entered her saucy lil' pussy. My left hand was still holding onto her panties as I placed my hardness at her entrance and coated the tip with her essence. I rubbed against her opening and occasionally pressed up against her clitoris. *Naked* by Marques Houston continued setting the mood after Boosie cut off. I slowly pushed my hardware into her center and she started to unarch her back, but I gently coerced her back into the proper position by placing my hand in the middle of her back and pushed down.

Once she adjusted to my length, she settled back into the proper position easily. Then I slow stroked her tight hole, loosening her up some more. I moved in and out of her, watching her pussy cream on my hard wood. I worked my way deeper inside her walls with her pussy greedily eating my hard-on, and I'm started to get lost in her sauce; I released the hold I had on her panties with my left hand and start working her from the back as I gripped her waist and thrusted myself inside her, slamming hard into her. The funny thing about this sexual situation is that I swear the perfect song came on at the right moment; the song that hit at that moment was that Gorilla Zoe joint *Juicebox*, so I put the hurtin' on her the best I knew how. I gripped her waist hard and started beatin' that box up. Shit was going good until I had to stop and remove her panties because they was rubbing my dick the wrong way.

With that, I had to pull my shit out and strip her out her drawers. I slipped them down to her knees and had her lie flat so I could take them the rest of the way off. Once I stripped her of her red panties, I wrapped them around my left arm, had her assume the proper position, smacked her on the left cheek, then grabbed myself with my right so I can get back to fucking. I pushed the head in then slid all the way, then I grabbed her waist and went back to working that pussy. I drilled her so good that it took some strength to hold her in place to keep her from running; I was afraid the police might be called the way I was murdering that box and the noise she was making didn't help. She creamed on my wood so much her name could've been Miracle Whip, which only fueled my sex rage. I pumped as fast and hard as my body allowed, then blew my load.

I left myself inside her and held onto her waist; she held me in place and threw her tight little ass back on my deflating hard on. It didn't help that she was looking back at me while she did it looking oh so sexy with those nerdy glasses. Plus, she claimed I was trying to break her pussy, which is impossible because I've tried. She did this until I went soft and slid out.
Afterwards, we headed to the shower to clean up but was interrupted by a phone call from my Pops. We walked to the bathroom while I talked on the phone; I had her prep the shower for us, and then she came back out while I talked. Pops and I talked for a few minutes and she was getting impatient, so while I talked, she got on her knees and started sucking me off. I started rising to the occasion and had to tell my O.G. that I'd hit him back because I had something to take care of. I hung up and we went inside the bathroom to handle round two.

Kassie Pt. 2

It was some time in early January of 2014 when Kassie came back to spend some time with me. What she didn't know at the time was that Lori and I had moved into my new apartment a few days ago, so what transpired was both a gift and a curse.

A call came through while I was at work from Kassie informing me I needed to pick her. This occurred during Christmas/New Year exodus that happens in the military, so it really was only half days of work, which made it all the more easier to leave and go pick up Kassie. I left the company office and drove to the airport and scooped Kassie up. Once I got there, I called her and let her know I was outside and was heading into grab her. She was sitting inside with a small travel bag, so I walked in and we greeted; she hugged me like she really missed me and I started to feel a rise in my uniform.

After a brief embrace and small talk, we walked out to the car. I still hadn't mentioned Lori was living with me, nor did I have a plan on what the hell I was gonna do, so I mentally said "fuck it" and waited to see how this was gone play out; either they would get along or not she was here now and I didn't think she'd reschedule her flight to turn around and leave the same day. Once we got to the car, I put her bag in, opened her door to let her in, closed it and walked around to get in. The drive from the airport to my apartment was less than five minutes away and I was a little nervous about bringing these two women together. Honestly, I figured since they both liked women that they would get along, at least that was my hope.

We arrived at my crib, park, and I grabbed the bag Kassie brought, then we proceeded to my apartment. The door was locked, so I used my key to get in. Lori was in the bedroom on the air mattress watching television; remember that we'd only moved in a few days ago, so there was no furniture in the house yet. Kassie and I entered the apartment, Lori came out, and I introduced them to each other. It was kind of awkward because I really hadn't told neither about the other, only because I had no intention of Lori moving in with me and Kassie and I had only been fucking for a few weeks, so I wasn't to concerned with filling either in on the other just yet.

Anyhow, like I said, I introduced them and let Lori know that Kassie was gonna be staying with us and that she was a friend. The fucked up thing was after I introduced them, I left and went back to work leaving them to get to know each other. Looking back on it I left two alpha females in my crib with all my possessions and full access to my apartment without any thought of the consequences, guess that what happens in the mind of a 25 year old. Things turned out pretty well in the end though.

Like I said, I left them after introductions and told them I'd be back later because I had things to do. Well, I get back to work and basically do nothing because it was the holidays and those who didn't take leave would work the mornings and be off at lunch time; we had only about two hours left of work, so I just sat at headquarters. While there I received texts from Lori telling me I was fucked up for what I did and how she was mad at me. I tried placating her and admitted I was wrong for not telling her about Kassie or the fact I was inviting someone else to my crib, which was now our crib. She let me know that it would have been okay if I gave her a heads up, but I didn't. After that, I got the silent treatment for the next hour or so, then before it was time to get off I received a text from Lori saying, " *We don't need you. We're getting along without you and having fun. Thanks.* "

That shit got me in my feelings. Here I was at work and these women were at my crib doing Allah knows what, and now they were acting like they didn't need me. I wanted to text her back and tell them both to get the fuck out, but I realized that would be the immature move, and although I could be immature at times I realized that this wasn't one of the time to act stupid. So, I thought through the situation; this could be another test as women constantly like testing us men, at least that's what the women in my family showed me. So, I text her back and said, *"I'm glad y'all are getting along. Keep having fun without me. I'll just go find me someone else to have fun with. Maybe Linda. lol. BTW, Imma go get ya'll a real bed so y'all can have* some *proper fun."* I did all that to flip to script on her and get her in her feelings.

Before I move forward, Linda was this thick, white woman I was occasionally smashing whom I met online; she was the type who wanted to be Black. Her and Lori met two days after I'd moved into my new spot. Lori and I had a disagreement, so she left and acted like she wasn't coming back. Me being me, I was like fuck it and let her go. I was already chopping it up with Linda anyhow, so after Lori left the house I went to see Linda at her place of work. Long story short, I invited Linda over to the apartment even though I had no furniture and we spent the night together on a pallet. We smashed and later on in the night Lori showed up and was trying to get in. I answered the door and told her I had some company and I thought she was gone, so why was she at my door. Dick move, I know, but I wasn't about to wallow in her leaving so I got under something else. Anyhow, she got to see my white girl, got in her feelings and left again, but only went next door to a 24 hour restaurant. I took Linda back to her place because she felt uncomfortable and didn't want any issues, then I went and made up with Lori.

Now back to our original story, my text only added fuel to the fire and she texted back talking about fucking all my shit up. This meant all my clothing, television, shoes, military gear, and electronics. I got slick at the tongue, so I text her back and said, " *If you fuck my shit up, Imma fuck you then fuck you up."* I knew she was 38 HOTT; she really hated that white girl and the fact I had her at "our" crib. She did that thing women do when they wanna test a man's gangsta, so she hit me with, *"You ain't gone do shit."* I had to make good on my word, so I left the office, hopped in my car, then headed home.

The drive home was short, about five minutes outside post. We lived in an efficiency apartment attached to a business that sold spas, so I parked around back and walked downstairs to my apartment. I took my keys, opened the door, and walked inside. No one was in the living room or kitchen, so I walked to the bedroom door and tried to go in, but it was locked. I knocked and calmly stated, " *Open the door. Don't try to hide now; what about all that shit you was talking on text."* They both started talking shit and laughing, which kind of pissed me off because I was locked outside my own room, but I didn't let it get the best of me. We went back and forth before they opened the door, and turned out they'd been day drinking and was lit already.

Lori was the one who opened the door and she stood there smiling and laughing her ass off; I was a little upset, but that dissipated when I saw how good she looked. We rarely kept on clothes in the house, but since company was around she had on a matching bra and panty set, purple in color, and I thought about making good on the first part of my text right there. After she opened the door laughing and smiling, she turned and went back to the air mattress; her ass was hanging out the back and that phat ass pussy poking out the front. Kassie was sitting on the bed nursing her drink and was still fully clothed, but those tight jeans fit her frame perfectly.

I was still light weight mad, so I played it up a little, and told them they better not lock any more fucking doors. As expected, they giggled and started talking shit. This was exactly what I wanted them to do, so I took off my uniform top while stating, *"Oh, y'all think this shit funny. Okay, I got something for dat ass."* I wanted to jump on her, but I knew the mattress wouldn't be able to handle that, so I casually sat on the bed next to Lori and pretended things were cool until they finished their drinks. It must had been fate, because Kassie got up to go in the bathroom. I waited until she went in the bathroom and closed the door, then I grabbed Lori's leg and pulled her towards me; she screamed and laughed as I "attacked" her. I pinned her down on the mattress and started giving her a hickey on her left breast. It didn't take her long to call for backup and Kassie came out of the bathroom after she'd done her business.

Kassie came out the bathroom to rescue her new friend and she grabbed me by my legs and tried to pull me off Lori. Being that I weighted more than her, it wasn't easy trying to pull me off Lori; it was akin to one of my children trying to pull me up off the couch or something. I rolled to the side and looked at Kassie like "what do you think you're doing" only to have that act as a distraction, because Lori started to assault me. She straddled me and sat on my chest; I felt the heat radiating from between her thighs and it felt as if my clothes wanted to burn off. I got turned on from seeing her semi nude and so close to my face I could smell her pussy. I mean she was already right there, so I tried to buck her closer to my mouth but she didn't move like I wanted her to; I would've ate that thang through the panties.

I pretended to fight back while Lori sat on my upper body and Kassie sat on my lower body; I thought we were about to all kiss and make-up since Lori was close to my face and Kassie was on my dick, even though she and I were still clothed. Nothing happened in that moment because the stupid air mattress started deflating from all our weight, so I knew it was time to go get some furniture. We all get up, Lori got dressed, and we headed out to find furniture for the house and pick up something to eat.

I decided to go to Rent-A-Center to get some furniture. A military court-martial was pending so there wasn't a need to pay full price when I was about to be confined in a few months. I wont bore you with all the details involved with getting the furniture. The gist of this part of the story is that we got there in time to get furniture, but I had to negotiate with the delivery guys so I could get it the same day because their delivery route was full before we arrived. In the end I got my furniture delivered, and that's where our story picks back up.

After being out all afternoon, we'd been sitting at home for about an hour waiting on the delivery of the bedroom and living room set. Initially, I thought they didn't have enough time and I'd have to wait until the next day, however, they arrived a little after 7 p.m. and that's when things got interesting to say the least.

I mentioned earlier that these women had been day drinking right? Well, after the delivery guys arrived they decided, for whatever reason, that they wanted to put on a show. This all started after they set up the living room with the two sofas, then moved to set up the bedroom set. Mind you that this was a small, efficiency apartment of about 900 square feet and it was now seven people in a small, confined space with four delivery guys putting together this bed frame, footboard, and headboard. Lori and Kassie took it upon themselves to start making out on the floor while these dudes tried to work. Imagine yourself trying to complete a job and two beautiful, yet tipsy, women making out and getting fingered; one has one nothing but panties and a T-shirt, while the other one is fully dressed but her pants fit so well that they looked painted on. No cap, I was a little embarrassed and turned on my damn self.

Here I was dealing with two liquored up alpha females, laughing, and having a girl-on-girl show in front of company. I managed to get them to get their shit together, but they decided to take the show to the bathroom. Now, instead of seeing the shit I got four guys plus myself in the room listening to one female getting ate out and moaning. They couldn't help but laugh. One of them even asked which one was my girlfriend, to which I replied *"both"* and I take it he didn't believe me because he just laughed and had this look of like "yeah, right!" I take it they were too distracted by the action in the bathroom, so I politely go in and inform them that they're gonna pay for this shit; however, whatever Kassie had done to Lori caused her to pass out. I guess she ate her pussy so good baby girl went to sleep

That left me with Kassie, who was still in a horny mood. She leaves and goes to the kitchen while I steady try to wake Lori up. She's passed out; I don't know if it's from the alcohol, the way Kassie ate her out, or a combination of both, but she wouldn't get up so I left her lying on the floor until the delivery crew finished assembling the bed. After leaving Lori alone, I go to the kitchen to talk to Kassie.

I entered the kitchen and Kassie was getting juice out the fridge. She's tipsy and in the mood, so she approached me trying to kiss on me while grabbing my dick. We walked towards the back wall and she whispered in my ear, "*I wanna suck your dick.*" I'm fighting with myself, on one hand I'm still in uniform and don't wanna be disrespectful to those who served before me, on the other I wanted to punish her and her mouth for the stunt they pulled. My inner beast won that battle, and I let her remove my growing erection from my uniform.

She takes me into her mouth. At first it's cold because of the juice she'd just consumed, but things heat up as she started pushing me further into her mouth; my member growing to it's full potential. Her pace was slow at first, then she started putting the hurt on me. I'm assuming not even ten minutes later the setup crew walked out my bedroom ready to leave, and they see me in the kitchen getting my rocks off. They all laugh and shake their heads; you know the joint where you're like "I can't believe this fool. He wild." That's the type of laugh and head shake they gave.

After they left I decided it was time to take matters into the bedroom. When we entered the bedroom, by what appears to be magic, Lori was out the bathroom and sitting in the new bed. Lil mama still drunk but coherent, and talking shit with that sexy ass smile of hers. Needless to say, I didn't get to finish the action from the kitchen, at least not yet. We all decide to sit in this new bed and kick it. Kassie kept asking Lori was she aight, and I was back to being ignored.
So, I grabbed my Kindle use it to switch on the TV and my Xbox, then put on some music. My dick was harder than Chinese arithmetic and I was beginning to be sexually frustrated, so I decided to walk next door to grab some more cigarettes. As I prepared to leave, Kassie asked me to pick up a pack of wraps.

I grabbed my phone and put on some warm clothes, then I walk out and dip to the convenience store next door and cop the items I wanted. Ya boy was still in his feelings about not getting no pussy, so while I was in the store I hit up Linda to see what was shaking. Shawty was off work, so I let her know I might slide through in a few so go head a freshen up for me.
After I paid for the cigarettes and wraps, I walked back to the crib. Upon opening the door, I already had planned to tell them I needed to go handle some business and that I was gone snatch some more liquor up for the weekend. They were still talking and laughing it up, so I dropped the wraps off and told them I'll be back in a few. They asked where I was going and

how long I'll be gone and I told them about an hour or so.

As I prepared to leave, Kassie asked if I knew where to get some "smoke" cuz she only had enough for one blunt. I made a mention I might know someone: she tried to give me some money but I told her I had it covered. What she didn't know is that I had another side piece whose cousin lived in the apartments up the street. Anyhow, I left and copped the smoke, then went to see Linda to scratch an itch.

I arrived at her spot and walked upstairs. I knocked and she came to the door in nothing but a bra and a barely there g-string. That ass was dumb dumb; she reminded me of the White girl who played Stevie in *The Parkers* television show, except her ass was bigger and phatter. She smiles and grabs me hand, and ushers me into the room. As we walk to the bedroom I feel my muscle start to strain against my boxer brief like a wild animal caged against its will; my underwear acting as a muzzle, and my erection striving to rip free of its enslavement. Once we enter her bedroom, I approach her from behind and once I'm close enough I pressed my body into hers. I whisper into her ear, *"Can you feel me?"*, then I nibbled the top of her ear, trailing my tongue down the side of her neck while breaking bodily contact.

She's too caught up in the moment to say anything, so I continue my course of action by caressing her body further pressing my fully erect dick in the small of her back, then I slipped my finger into her pussy as I whispered, *"Can you feel me now?"* I don't know why she chose that moment to say what she said, but she almost ruined my mood because she decided to mention Lori and why I ain't with her right now. I casually brushed her off and told her that I'm here with her and let`s focus on the right now. She wanted to push the issue, so I removed my hand from her pussy, turned her around, and pushed her on the bed.

I reached down and removed her g-string and slide between her thighs. My hands left hand found its way into her hair, and I pull it causing her to tilt her head and slightly arch her back. My lips kiss her right cheek and I place little kiss down her body until I reach her breasts.
Somehow, through all this, this bitch still on that same shit. Here I am setting the mood and she worried bout my main. As I suck on her left titty, she tells me either I leave Lori and be with her or this the last time we fuck. I'm ready to jet at this point, so I get up, unzip my jeans and pull my shit out. I wasn't looking to put it down anymore, so I slide my shit in and go to work from the missionary position. My goal now is to punish her, then get the hell outta dodge.

As I'm stroking her thick ass, all I'm focused on is her pussy talking to me and her labored breathing. I'm enjoying piping her up, so I grabbed her legs and push them towards her head. **My** chocolate dick looked damn good penetrating her little white pussy, and I enjoyed my last fuck. Things got juicy and I focused on getting my nut. At this point her pussy felt like it was pulling me deeper into her warm depth; the feeling of ecstasy coming in wave after wave, drowning me--calling for me to just give up and let her wetness consume me. I give in and let the kids run wild. My shit still hard after dropping my load, so I continue to stroke her inside letting our juices mix together. After I'm satisfied, I pull out and give her a quick peck on the cheek, thanking her for the release.

I get up and prepare to do a quick clean-up: wash my dick in the sink with a rag, soap, and water. Somehow, yet again, shawty still on leaving my girl for her. I let her know that's not gone happen, so she lets me know that was our last time having sex and she heads to the shower and told me I can let myself out. So, I finished my business and headed to post so I could re-up on the liquor. I've been gone for about forty minutes by now, so when I got in the whip I had a couple texts from the girls asking where I was at and when I'd get home. I hit them both back and let them know I'll be there in30, I'm almost done handling business.

I peel out Linda's parking lot and made my way to the base. Once on-post I grab a few bottles of Henny, Peach Ciroc, some Raspberry Schminoff for Kassie, some chaser (Red Bull and Crangrape), and a carton of Newports because we all smoked them. I prepared to head to checkout, not really paying attention, I heard someone call my name and I look up and an associate of mine's was working the cash register. It was this female name Eisha, who was the sister of another female I knew through a third party. Anyhow, she called me over to her register and rung my stuff up. We made conversation and flirted with each other. I would've smashed a long time ago, but she was messing with this white boy I knew. Shawty reminded me of a sexier Solange Knowles but with a Memphis twist. All in all, she hooked me up on the spread and I left.

My drive back to the crib was short and I arrive home less than five minutes. After parking next to the bedroom window, I hop out and I hear the music still going from earlier. I made my way round to the stairs and descend to my front door, then let myself in. They're still in the room with the door closed, so I take the liquor in the kitchen, down two shots and pour up a Henny and Red Bull. Now, I don't know if they planned this shit or not, but as I open the door I see Kassie straddled across Lori; she had both of Lori's hand pinned in hers and they were kissing. If I recall, I believe Field Mob's *"Dead in yo Chevy"* was playing on my XBox music, so

I grabbed my Kindle and switched it to some Twista. The sight was a turn on, so I casually walked around the bed to get a better view of the show. They're enjoying themselves, and Kassie eventually found her way down south. Lori already told me she was bisexual, so I was hoping something like this was gone pop off this weekend, even though I'd fucked up. Anyhow, Kassie slid Lori's underwear to the side and went to work. I thought I ate the box good, but the show she put on and the noises Lori made had a nigga feeling a lil' insecure, but that quickly passed. I sat back and watched the show for a while and nursed my drank. I know I'd just fucked Linda about an hour ago, but I was ready to go again. Simply watching Lori get her pussy ate while Kassie's ass was arched up towards my face made me take my drink to the head and try to join the festivities.

I stood up and walked behind Kassie, then I lightly slapped her ass through her jeans. Next, I press my growing hard-on to her ass and grinded a little to let her know I was enjoying their show. After doing that stunt, I moved back and removed my pants then stood there in my boxer briefs. My initial attempt to join the fray was thwarted as I tried to help Kassie take off her pants; this broad tried to tell me her period was on. I went along with it for the moment and proceeded to engage with Lori. I lie on the bed beside both of them and start kissing on Lori's collarbone and make my way to her breasts. I suck on her left breast while Kassie polish her peach, but I'm pushed away; I get the hint so I let them do their thing since I'd already got one off. I walked out and refilled my empty glass, then came back to watch the show.

I stood off in the corner watching these two beauties go at it; Lori expressing her pleasure loudly as she usually does, and Kassie expertly devouring Lori's phat cat. I sat there stroking myself with my left hand and sipping my drink with my right. They go at it for another ten minutes or so, then I try to get in on the action again; I try removing Kassie's jeans again and was rebuked with her previous answer of her period on while pushing my hands away, so instead I decide to see what she was doing to make Lori moan like that. She had a lip lock on the clit and was working that lil' motherfucker. I decided I wanted to help so I slip two finger in Lori and massage her insides. After a while, Lori bucked on my fingers and Kassie's face. After that, she got up, went to the bathroom, and locked the door; all we heard after that was water running.

Since they're through with their freak-fest, Kassie finally asked me where the smoke was at I get up to grab the pack from the liquor bag in the kitchen. My nigga told me it was called "mac'n cheese". After grabbing the pack, the rest of my Henny and her vodka, I head back to the room. I pass her the gas and her bottle, then I strip down to my birthday suit. Shawty got the wraps and rolled up while I searched the music for something to get lit to. I replayed Twista's " *Kill'em All"* and let his discography play. Kassie finished rolling up the blunt, cuddled up beside me, then sparked up. It has been some years since I last smoked, but at this point I didn't care, so I hit that shit along with her.

While we smoked, Lori sat her ass in the bathroom soaking in the tub. We smoked, dranked, and kicked the shit while Lori did her. Before I knew it, I was sky high, and my body felt like it was in tune with every beat that came on; ya boy was vibin' the hell out. I was so gone, I didn't realize Kassie removed her pants: she had on some yellow laced panties, and her period wasn't even on! I know because she straddled me while *"Chocolate Fe's and Redbones"* was on and ground her pussy against me while in the reverse cowgirl position. She was working that lil ass on me like we was actually fucking. This bitch even had the nerve to lean over on her elbows, look back at me, and twerk a little. I was gone, but not that gone, so I reached and hooked her panties; she backed up on me like she was ready for some action, so I slipped one finger inside her when she started throwing it back on my finger like she had a dick in her. That sent me over the edge and I was ready to strike sum.

She's so entranced by the music, I don't think she realized I'd moved my finger outta her soaking wet pussy cuz she was still twerking to the music like she was on a pole; once again I had my own lil' private dancer. I take this time to slide my legs from under her and knee my way behind her. She tried to move, but I gripped her waist and let her feel my shit was hard as a motherfucker and I was done playing games for the night. I was about to punch a hole in her drawz on some real nigga shit, but she acquiesced and leaned down and arched her back.

I take the time and remove her panties, with her assistance. In front of me is a glistening pussy, wet and ready for penetration. I reach down and grab my dick and place the head of my erection near her entrance. I hold it there firmly like a snake ready to strike at any moment--my dick was fully hard, veined, and my head flared like a viper's hood and the tip leaking venom. She moved cautiously against my manhood, but I struck suddenly, biting into her insides causing our fluids to mince together. As I let this snake crawl deeper in her hole, her body starts to weaken; she gripped the covers and held on for the ride, no longer throwing it back like she was before we started fucking. If she thought we was gone put in the work, she was in for a surprise that night.

I pull out and lie back down on the bed with my member pointed skyward like the Tower of Babel. She had the nerve to say, *"Nigga! Why you stopped? I was about to cum!"* I told her that since she lied about her period being on, she was gone have to do all the work tonight, and told her that she was gone fuck me in the same reverse cowgirl position she teased me in. Truth be told, I was too fucked up to hit that ass from the back, but she ain't have to know that. Whatever the case, she took it in stride as she backed her ass up, straddled me, and climbed on that stick. She took me in like a champ and as usual I felt enough resistance that I knew she couldn't take no more; she was full.

She rode me like a cowgirl's supposed to. That pussy had a vacuum seal on my staff while she used my legs for support. Our sex created a good mixture of pleasure; at first it sounded like a freshly cracked egg being released in a bowl, then once it got good it was akin to beating eggs in a bowl with a fork--at least that's what my high ass mind thought of at the time. I was so caught up in how good the sex was I was trying to stuff her some more but kept hitting her backstop, but that didn't stop me as I pushed up in her while she rode me. I eventually shoot my load and Kassie rolled off me, her feet facing my face; she laid there rubbing her pussy.

Lori was still in the bathroom at this point, and I'm sure she heard us in there fucking, but I didn't care. I felt like she was in her feelings, and I was a young nigga bout to get locked up, so I was carefree. That's why after smashing Kassie I got up and rolled that last blunt; it had been a while since I rolled, but ya boy from GA and you know how we gets down. Once I finished rolling, I sparked it up and changed my music to some Tupac. I tried passing it to Kassie, but she was good, so I solo'd that shit til about halfway. When I finished, I was ready to wash the pussy scent off me, so I try to enter to bathroom, but it was still locked. I asked Lori to open the door but she was in her feelings still. I wasn't playing game anymore, so I found something and jimmied my way into the bathroom.

The lights were off, and she was sitting there with candles lit, soaking in the tub. I thought about getting in the tub, but I decided to let the toilet seat down and sit there. The goal was to try and have a conversation to smooth shit over, but things didn't go that way. I did all the talking and was met with the silent treatment. No matter how much I turned the charm on I was met with the cold shoulder, so I decided to get in the tub with her, and she let me. I slide in the water behind her, and we sit there and soak. I try again to get a conversation started, but nothing elicits much from her, although she did let me hold her and even attempt to strum the kitty with my fingers. All in all, she simply told me she was mad at me, then she got out the tub, dried off and left me solo dolo.

I didn't want her to blow my high, so I let the water out and ran some more, then flicked the lights on while I stepped out to grab my bottle of Henny, Newports, and the unfinished blunt. It was time to relax, so I fucked around and made me a bubble bath, clicked the lights off and left the candles lit. I grabbed the ashtray off the counter and hopped my ass in the tub. When I got in the tub, I realized I needed something to set the mood so I called Kassie in and asked her to grab my iPod and deck out the kitchen. As I waited for her I spark the blunt up and toked that joint. My mind, body, and soul felt relaxed as I inhaled and held the smoke; the warmth in my chest traveling through my body being amplified by the heat from the water as the bubbles lapped against my body.

A few seconds later Kassie comes in with the requested items, and I asked her to hit playlist "GaFinest"; this had a majority of my favorite artists from round the way, i.e. Outkast, Field Mob, Goodie Mabb, Cyhi, Jody Breeze, and more. *"Black Ice"* by Goodie Mob was the first song to blast the airways. If you're a fan, you know that shit slap when the first verse hit:

Now you know, and I know, I done bumped every hole in the wall ya'll. Did you catch that phone call? Most of y'all dat met me thought I was tall. Get flipped like ip, slipped fell on that black ice. Did you think twice? Homes/ice, came and he went satisfied. Got bent, bars ain't shit. Mutin' coast to coast, yeah I loved dem both, mad dose to dose, too *many comin' close...*

I might've fucked up some of the words, but you catch the drift. Anyhow, I passed the blunt and we finished that thang off while I sat my tall ass in the tub. Shawty wanted to have a conversation, but I wasn't trying to get into all that at the time, so she just left it at I need to talk to Lori. After Kassie left I sat there smoked a Port, and sipped a lii' sum. Last thing I recall was letting some water out, adding more hot water and some more soap, then I fucked around and passed out in the tub. When I woke up, the water was lukewarm and most of my bubble had disappeared; I'd been gone for about an hour. After that power nap I was feeling extraordinary, so I hit my body twice over and got out. I grab all my vices and head to the bedroom to dry off.

Since I've been out for an hour, I figured at least things were cordial, but that wasn't the case as I dried off and tried to speak to Lori again while she was curled up on the bed naked pretending to be sleep. I let her have her moment, and grabbed my Georgia Tech pajamas and slid them on. By this time I was hungry, so I left to fix me a sandwich. As I left the bedroom, Kassie was on the couch in the living room scrolling through Netflix. She told me we needed to talk, so I told her give me a minute while I fix me something. I turn the oven on and fix my roast beef sandwich. After I'm done, I throw the sandwich-in aluminum foil--in the oven to toast it, then I go see what Kassie wanted to discuss.

Turns out her and Lori **talked** while I was passed out in the tub. I had to grab my food before we went down that rabbit hole, so I also poured up another drink. Long story short, she told me that Lori was in love with me, that I should've told her I had someone else living with me, and how I needed to make it right with Lori. I knew she was right, but it hurt hearing how bad I fucked up. I told her since she couldn't find anything to watch to put on the Arnez J standup, then I went back to the bedroom to try once again to repair the situation.

I entered the bedroom and Lori was still curled in the fetal position on the bed, her ass facing me. I closed the door and kneeled next to the bed, then I did what I do best which was turn on the charm. My left hand found its way to her hip and I asked her was she up, which I knew she was; she pretended to be sleep, so I lightly shook her and asked her again was she up. She pushed my hand off and slid away from me towards the middle of the bed. That didn't deter me, so I simply climbed in with her and wrapped my arm all the way around her waist. We were laid in the spoon position, and she was "awake" now. She tried removing my arm, but there wasn't any real action behind it. This let me know I at least had her attention, so I let my death grip go.

Once I release her, I take the time to remove her hair from around her face and place it behind her ear, then I start by telling her how sorry I am for hurting her. This leads into a whole spiel about how I know she loves me, how I was selfish for springing Kassie on her, why I did it, and so on. Throughout this ordeal I could feel the tension leave her body and her start to soften up to my touches. I ended my monologue by telling her even though Kassie wasn't supposed to leave until Monday that I'd pay to have her ticket scheduled to leave tomorrow if she wanted me to. I was hoping that wasn't the case, but I was willing to do whatever to fix the relationship. Turns out she didn't want Kassie to leave because she turned and told me, *"You not sending my friend away because you fucked up. Plus I really like her, she's a cool chick."* I assumed she was poking fun at me cuz she also add she liked the way Kassie at her out.

All I could say was I'm glad she got something out the deal, which earned me a kiss; I knew I was in there after that. This lead to us sharing a passionate kiss leading to the "young one" waking up ready to join the party. I disengaged from our kissing and started trailing kisses down her arm then back up to her shoulder where I found myself tonguing Lori down again. My guy was fully ready, so I stopped kissing and rolled outta bed where I removed my pj's. Lori rolled over and looked at me as I stripped naked. My shit was standing straight out so I made it jump like when a high diver leaps off the diving board. After eliciting a laugh tram her, I crawl back into the bed and give Lori a quick peck. Next, I ask her to roll back onto her side. From there I remove her hair from her shoulder and nibble on it.

From there my lips plant kisses down her spine as I trailed my way to the dimples in her lower back. I push on her slightly and she responds by turning over just enough to give me access to both cheeks. Starting on her right side, my tongue leaves a small trail of saliva as I move towards her left side crossing the top of her ass. As I reached her left hip I kiss and suck on her left ass cheek causing her to arch and open up to me; I repeat this performance on the right side. She's moaning and enjoying the show I'm putting on. Once I finished spending time on her right cheek I move myself towards the top of her tailbone. I kiss and roll my tongue around the split of her ass, then blow on it, teasing her. Next, I slide my tongue between her split without breaking the seal, only licking outside; I feel the heat erupting from her pussy as I make my way towards the cusp of her cheek.

Once I reach where her ass naturally cups, I take my hand and spread her open taking a deep inhale of her intoxicating scent. Her pussy was sweet and coated in its natural honey; the heat emanating from her center reminded me of going to grandma's house for Sunday dinner and she had it smelling hella good off up in there, then you walk in the kitchen to see what's cooking and you smell something sweet in the oven knowing it's that Jiffy cornbread but you open the oven anyhow, and the heat along with the scent of the cornbread hits you in the face causing your eyes to close and your mouth to water. This made me lick her from the bottom of her opening to her clit, leaving her with a small peck after doing so. It's go time after that because my dick was leaking precum and felt like it was about to explode.

I lie down in the spoon position and prepare to enter Lori. I take my left hand and lift her ass cheek and she responds by opening up and guides my erection home. Usually I'd fuck her real good from this position, but that night I took the time to make love. For the next forty minutes or so we went from spooning, to her laying on her stomach, and ending up in the missionary position. That night felt better than any other time we'd had sex. As I prepared to cum, my dick felt like it was in a cave and the walls were closing in on me--choking the life from my body. I struggled to breathe and climb out, but her cave somehow drew me deeper and deeper until at last I drew my final breath and released everything left in me as she constricted me from all sides. I felt a sense of peace like never before as I laid there, limp and unmoving, my manhood still inside her.

I laid there on top of her and she held me, tears flowing from her eyes. I thought I'd done something wrong so I asked what was up and why she was crying, she said " *Nothing's wrong fool. I'm crying because I love you so much. And that's the first time you made love to me."* That made me feel good, but also think about all the times we'd had sex, then I realized she was right; a few times started out as love making but then it turned to something else. I made a silent promise to myself to be a little more gentle. After giving her a kiss I rolled off and she snuggled up in my arms and we laid there as she threw her legs over me and her arms over my chest.

A couple minutes later Kassie comes in and tells us, " *Damn, bout time y'all done. I been waiting wash my ass girl."* Lori laughed, grabbed my face, and kissed me; I now realize that was her subtle way of claiming ownership. In the end we all washed our asses and ended up all sleeping in the same bed. Overall, the weekend was pretty damn good even though I didn't get a real three-way. Monday afternoon I took Kassie to the airport and we parted ways as friends only from that point. Even her and Lori stayed in touch as friends, so I felt like that's a win in my book.

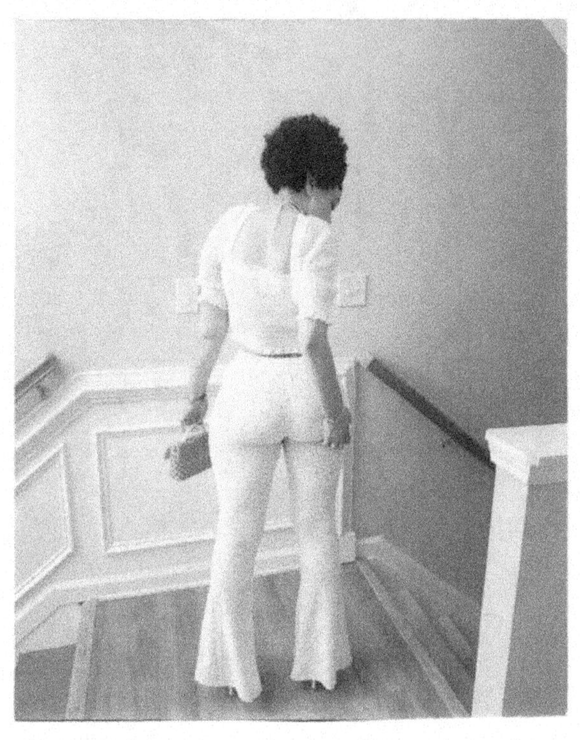

Carmen

"Ibe fucking broads, like I be fucking bored. Turn a dike chick out, have her fucking boys."
A$AP Rocky; *Fuckin' Problem*

This story has been changed to protect this woman's identity because I don't want any kickback in whatever career she's decided to take up, nor do I want to prevent opportunities from coming her way because of the release of this story. I don't express this story to brag as I could've chosen other stories for that; I chose to write about this story because of the indelible impression she left on me and the notion that some lesbians still need and want the real thing.

Carmen was a mutual friend of the family and wore stereotypical lesbian attire: low-fade and baggy clothing, but underneath her masculine facade I saw a beautiful woman; there are some things you can't hide no matter how hard you try. Her skin was the color of cinnamon with physical features that were hard to hide from my eyes. She stood about 5' 6", and I felt she had curves like a country back road: it was like Billie Eilish trying to hide her breasts even though you know they're there and big as a bounce-house. It turned out she had 0-cup breasts- yes lawd- and a nice wide, phat booty, with sexy ass lips like Diamond DeShields or Destanni Henderson. Anyhow, we didn't start out as friends or lovers until a year or so after meeting.

We met in 2012 after I'd returned from Afghanistan on my second deployment. The first deployment was easy, but this one changed me in a way I didn't realize until it was too late, which is a story in and of itself. At the time, I came back to the woman who birthed my kids and wanted to live right. We were staying together at the time and it turned out that she'd made some friends while I was gone. I'd spoken with two female friends via Skype while deployed, which I believed was a setup I didn't fall for even though they were fuckable. The weekend of my return, my BM (baby mama) threw me a welcome home party and invited all her little friends over; they were all cute, even the two big girls. I played nonchalant with everyone because my woman was the jealous type, but I quickly scoped out Carmen and felt some kind of connection even with her dressed like a dude.

Eventually we connected over our love of Henny and music, but I kept the rest at a distance. Like I said, we didn't become lovers overnight. Carmen continued to grow on me as she continually came to the crib where we hosted kickbacks. At one particular party we were talking and she showed me a photograph of her back in high school when she was still girly, and I was blown away by the transformation. Not only was she gorgeous back in the day, but it was like a total 180 in looks. Now I knew shorty was bhad bhad, but you couldn't really tell it upon initial looks. I lightweight got upset that she'd cut her hair and went to the extreme of hiding her beauty. In my mind I wanted to make a move on her because I felt the vibes, but I was in a committed relationship, and as I said, I was looking to make it work with the mother of my children.

Fast-forward to late 2013 and the people we once partied with had split off due to an incident where one of my pool tables were broken through drunken misbehavior. Long story short, I made the culprit pay for it, they got mad, wanted to fight me and my BM, and we wasn't having that, so we parted ways and I kept the money anyhow. Things popped of with me and Carmen on a Friday in September of 2013 when one of my Brothers and I decided to go out together because we'd been "Raised" a few months ago. I felt a break was needed from the BM and the drama she was stirring up about me cheating, when at the time I wasn't. Turned out she was the perpetrator, and with no other than the same so called "brother" I'd went out with. That's a song for another time.

On this particular Friday night, me and my Square were drinking at our respective cribs. I hit him up and asked if he wanted to go out and hit the town. He was down for the cause, so I hit the shower and got low-key fresh to death. I dressed in my black Lo (Polo Ralph Lauren) boots; slim fit Ambercrombie blue jeans; Ralph Lauren belt; a multicolored green Ralph Lauren short- sleeved button up; a black tie; a black Ralph Lauren V-neck sweater; some Ralph Lauren Explorer cologne; a white Polo cap with the Black horse; and of course my Ralph Lauren shades. I was on my Tiger Woods and Young Dro shit.

About 9 'clock, I jumped in my truck and drove to the Class VI and snatched up a bottle of Henny, a pack of Newports and some Wine Black & Mild's, a 6-pack of Red Bull, and some Ciroc for my bro. Afterwards, I drove around the comer to his crib and we pregamed until about eleven. Once we're on lean, we hopped in his Lincoln truck and headed out on the town to relieve some stress and cut loose. Our first stop was the local country club, as they sometimes played Hip-Hop/Rap music, but we don't discriminate because good music is good music, am I right?

The parking lot was full, so we looked for a spot to park. We were finally able to take the spot of a Black Nissan Maxima leaving out. He parked the truck and we went inside. The place was packed like sardines and it wasn't even Hip-Hop night. Once inside he saw some people he knew and we hung tor a while. The DJ was spinning some good music, i.e., Tim McGraw, Keith Urban, and even some Kenny Chesney; we even got on the floor and line danced with some of the people. We stayed for like an hour doing Jell-0 shots with some white girls, then we headed out to see what else was shaking.

We hit several clubs that night, but ended up staying for a while in this spot that was more akin to a hole-in-the-wall joint; it was part strip club and actual club. This place also had a packed parking lot, and we ended up parking at the local extended stay hotel and walking over. Once there, we paid to get in and grabbed a few Coronas; he sparked a Newport and I sparked a Wine Black & Mild I've been babysitting throughout the night. We didn't stay too long because the actual club part was about to close, so we decide to check out the strip club for a while. On the way out the door I bumped into Carmen and we chopped it up for a while. She was ecstatic to see me as it had been some time since we last hung. She greeted me with a hug and for some reason my shit started to get hard; I hoped she didn't really notice, but I later found out she did. Nolie, I felt the vibes in the air and after kicking the shit, we decided to link at the Rockin' Rodeo club.

Carmen left while we went next door to the strip club. We entered the joint and there's this pretty ass woman sitting at the door taking the entry fee, so we pay and go in. The place is okay, but way too small, and the women were not all that nice looking. We go to the bar and I order a Henny and Sprite plus a Corona and my dude orders just a beer. We chill at the bar scoping the scene, and he sees some dancer he knows and they go to a table and she starts to dance on him in the dark corner. I'm left to my own device so I keep surveying the place. After a while I decide to talk to the lady at the door because she was one of the better looking women in there besides this mixed chick who danced there.

I walk over, introduced myself, and asked to sit in the other chair then proceed to sit down before she answered. She's engaged in taking money from patrons entering the door, so I'm getting no play at the moment. I keep making conversation because I'm not one to be intimidated by a little cold shoulder. I let her know that she's cute, but she ain't all that, with her nose in the air. Then I tell her that either her feet or her breath probably stinks and that's the reason she has her nose in the air and face scrunched up, which elicits a laugh. Now I'm getting somewhere. I finally learned her name was Monica, she was 32 with two kids, with one on the way, and a single mother. At the time I was only 25, but we still exchanged numbers after our conversation.

After some time, I get bored of this little strip joint as I've met a new potential friend and there's nothing shaking in this spot. Literally, the women were petite with no asses, maybe a butt, but definitely no ass. We end up popping smoke from there to head to the Rockin' Rodeo. We hopin the truck and head to the club, but before we get there we make a pitstop to re-up on smokes and fuel. Afterwards, when we pull up to the spot, it's jam packed as well. If you haven't guessed by now, it's payday weekend, so everybody and their mother was out. The line's super long, it's cold as apolar bear's asshole, and people were hopping out at the door just to hold spots for friends. Luckily for us we knew people working the door, so we didn't have to wait too long, and boy was people mad.

Once we get in and pay the $20 entry fee: for some reason it's higher than usual but whatever. The club was divided into sections: one for Rap/Hip-Hop, one for Country and karaoke, and one for Pop music. We all head upstairs to the Hip-Hop section, get some drinks and find a few tables. The ones we found were close to the dance floor. As I settle in at the table, Carmen and her crew pull up behind us and ask to join, which we welcome. I'm sipping my Henny straight and start vibin' to the music. The floor was packed so it was no need for me to be out there, plus I had to get a scope of what was going on because you never know what could pop off at these spots, even with security. I'm big chillin' and groovin' to Pastor Troy as the DJ amps the club up with "Vice Versa". I'm in my zone, but Carmen's trying to get my attention. She's making hand signals that are hard to see in this dark place, even though she's few feet in front of me.

I stop what I'm doing to lean in to see what she wanted. She plants a kiss right on my lips, and I go with the flow; however, I notice the other hoes watching. I'm thinking my **BM** definitely gone find out, but fuck it. It's over just as quick as it started, and I knew it was gonna be on tonight. Anyhow, she wanted my lighter, but what she didn't know was that she'd light a fire somewhere else. I give her the lighter and go back to playing it cool, all the while plotting on how and where Imma smash. While I was plotting on Carmen, someone else was plotting on me. There was a woman standing in my peripheral cutting her eyes at me, but I pretended not to notice. As I told you I was low-key fresh to death on my Tiger Woods and Young Oro shit. This woman took notice, and she "accidentally" bumped me while I was about to sip my drink. She apologizes, asks if I'd like another, and then proceeds to tell me how much she like my 'fit. I later find out her name was Cortencie and she kind of resembled the actress Ebony Obsidian, who plays Karen on the television show *"Sistas"*. Nothing became of the situation, but she did have the softest lips I've had the pleasure of kissing, at the time.

The whole atmosphere for the night was on ten. I'd gotten two numbers and a woman who identified as lesbian pushed up on me, what more can a man ask for? We partied the night and morning away until the club let out. After last call, we cleared out and prepared to go back to our homes. We hop in bruh's truck and The Game's song "Church" is knocking through the speaker; I took that as a sign that I had to slice up Carmen tonight. Why? Because at the time she was a chaplain's assistant. On our way back to post, I hit Carmen up to see if she had other plans for the night because J had intentions of sliding through. She replied she had nothing else planned besides going back to the barracks. I reply back and told her to hit me when she arrived, then I let her know that "we" thinking about her

We made it back to post safely without any accidents or DUI's. He drove us back to his crib and I received a message from Carmen asking me am I coming through because she at the B's (barracks). I tell her yeah, we just pulled up and I'm about to head over in about ten minutes. We sit at the curb of his crib, I hit the autostart on the whip, and I inform bro that if my **BM** asked then I'm with him, typical bro code shit. We sit for about two or three minutes, smoke a cigarette, and I get in my whip and made my way towards Carmen.

It's about 3 in the morning when I get to the B's and park by her car. Once there, I text her that I arrived. She tells me to come in through the side entrance, she's already propped it open. I kill the ignition, hop out, and make my way to the side entrance, but once I get there it's locked. My first instinct is that she trying to play me, but I hit her back and let her know that the door isn't open. She let's me know she'll be there in a few. So I'm waiting at the door, in the snow, like some creep, hoping no one I know sees me, because I didn't need extra problems at that point. Eventually she comes down and opens the door and we make our way to her room. She's in a white beater and some boy shorts and I watch her ass try to stay contained as we walk the stairs. I couldn't help but smack that thang one time, it would've been disrespectful not to; she laughed and told me to wait til we get in the room. We arrived without incident and make our way inside.

The lights are low and she has candles burning, it smelled good as a motherfucker. She asked if I wanted something to drink, to which I took some water. She's nervous and I can tell, so I move to her bed and take off my sweater and boots, she comes over and assists me in removing the latter. Once I'm comfortable I lie down on her lap and we talk for a while. It's hard to stay focused on the conversation with her breasts spilling out of her white beater, so I occasionally bite them, lightly though. Other than that, conversation is smooth and we're in a groove like we been together for a while; her holding me in her lap, occasionally kissing my lips.

and caressing my face while we converse.

I know time is of the essence since I've been out all night, and I can't just stay here and play house with Carmen. I sit up and get out the bed, stand between her legs and slide her towards me. I lean down and kiss her on those luscious lips of hers and grab her ass letting her know that I've been wanting her for along time. She informs me that she's been feeling me for a long time as well, then asks me how my baby mama gone feel about me being out all night. I let her know that I've got that under control and that she needs to worry about what we have going on right here, right now. I know she only asked because my **BM** was a crazy Leo, and a whole lot of hood in her; Carmen wasn't built like that so I know she didn't want anything to complicate her life.

I haven't rocked up yet, but things start to get intense and Carmen suggests we hit the shower. I stand and strip naked right there in the middle of her room and she does the same. I think it caught her by surprise when she saw me naked, because she said *"why's it little?"*. I laughed and told her *I promise you it gets bigger,* I guess she was used to the "showers" not "growers" when she saw my soft 37/8 inch penis. After settling that problem, she grabs my hand and leads me to the shower. She turns the water on and set it toa comfortable temperature, then we jump in. Carmen begins by washing me letting her hand linger near my penis as she washes me with the other. There's a lustful look in her eyes and I knew I had it in mines as well. After she gives me a good washing I step in front of the shower head to rinse the soap off while she gives herself a clean. As she's washing her body I can't help but notice how amazing her body looks naked: beautiful brown breasts bouncing as she washes them, clean- cut coochie, and a delicately delicious looking derriere.

I step out of the way so that she can wash off, but not before giving her my signature grin. As she's washing off, I'm staring at her backside, and the way her pussy sat between her thighs. I was like a hungry tiger eyeing its prey and I get one of the strongest erections of my life. While she's facing forward, I walk up behind her and poke her backside. She turned around and sees my hard on and says,"*I guess* you *were right When you said it gets bigger,"* then she pushes me toward the back of the shower, takes me into her hands, goes to her knees and starts bopping me off. It feels good, but I've never gotten off that way, EVER. After a while I pull out and reach down to help her up so that I can return the favor

I guided her to the back wall, and I squat down between her legs and inhale her scent. She smelled wonderful, which made my mouth water; I love pleasing a woman, but I don't eat out all the time. Carmen was the fifth person I'd ever went down on. Water was splashing on my back, my mouth watered, and her pussy looked good enough to quench my thirst. I give that pretty brown mound a quick kiss, then I look up at her expectantly. She opened up wider for me so I go in for a better sample. Honestly, I was nervous at first because I'd never encountered pussy lips like hers during any of my sexual encounters; the labia minora hung and I had to work to get to the clitoris, but when I did she had a sweetness to her.

She had to have felt powerful with me eating her in the "all hail the queen" position. I could tell from the way she held my head, the lustful look in her eyes, and the way she rode my face; I'm all for women empowerment, but I knew it was time to retake control of the situation while still pleasing the lady. So I take her on an elevator ride to the top floor. I honestly don't know where the strength came from because even though I was athletic I wasn't strong and muscular as I am now that I'm older. You also have to consider that I was 6' 5", so she was at least ten feet in the air given her height of 5' 6", and I'm going to town on that pussy in the shower. I forgot to mention that before we started all this that she told me that she doesn't get wet like that for dudes, which turned out to be a lie.

Like I said, I found the strength to lift this woman and take her on an elevator ride, which had always been on my "fuck it" list. I was enjoying myself and she was as well since she messed up my waves. When she got off on the top floor, pun intended, I put her down and we went into her bedroom and decided to dry off. Afterwards, she laid on the bed spread-eagle and I moved forward and rubbed myself against her opening. At first it seemed like she'd grown dry on me just that quick and that maybe she'd told the truth about not getting wet, but that quickly changed with some tongue action. Once she was lubricated up, I penetrated her soft outer flesh and after about seven or eight strokes I was coated in her thick cream. Ya boy was putting the pound game down proper in the missionary, but I definitely had to hit that from the back before I dropped my load. Not hitting that ass from the back who have been akin to getting to smash Chloe Bailey or Megan thee Stallion and never giving them proper back shots.

So I pulled out, my dick lathered in thick cream, and asked her to roll over on all fours. Once she was on all fours I grabbed another taste of that pussy before I dove back in, and she still tasted sweeter than cane sugar; I could've lived down there. I sampled the pussy for about a minute, to allow myself time to recover from how good her pussy felt, and I reentered her like a thief in the night. I crept in real slow, giving her shallow strokes, then put it all the way in. Once I was fully in, I sat there flexing my muscle inside her. Next, I rotated my hips in a circular motion like I was mixing cake batter. She was enjoying the teasing and even teased me back by following my rotations and occasionally throwing it back. What she didn't know was that if we had kept up this little charade a little longer I would've blew my load early, so to prevent that I pull out again and had her climb in the bed facing the headboard so I could get in too.

I climbed into the bed with her facing the headboard, still in the doggy position. Carmen didn't have a phat cameltoe but that pussy still looked amazing while she was face down ass up. Looking back on it, she had the perfect arch in her back for a lesbian when I was trying to knock that out the frame. Anyhow, I pull up behind Carmen and enter her once more. I'm on my knees using leverage from her hips to penetrate her gushy center as well as my core muscles. It didn't take long to get back into a rhythm where I'm long stroking her, she's throwing it back, and we're both making sounds of pleasure. She seemed to get wetter, so I literally had to stand up in it at one point. I mean feet pressed into the mattress, hands on her hips, and me dive bombing her pussy. Carmen loved that shit so much I had to tell her to grab the pillow because in my mind she was being too loud. We didn't need the person on duty to walk by and hear us fucking late night, especially since I wasn't supposed to be there in the first place, and I didn't check in at the front desk.

, I eventually succumb to her juiciness and release my essence inside her walls. The story doesn't end there though. After I relieve myself I draw my sword out of her sheath, I slid my back to the footboard; dick still hard, legs wide, drawn out and open. Even with the scented candles burning, you could smell good sex in the air, so Carmen decides she wasn't finished and slides between my legs and pops me in her mouth. Now you know us men are extremely sensitive down there after ejaculating, plus she played around at the tip, and I damn near jumped out my skin. I think she just wanted me to lie my legs straight because once I did she straddled me quickly, like we were doing combatives, and placed my still erect penis into her vagina.

This woman rode me like an experienced equestrian with her bodacious breasts in my face and hands around my neck for support. I couldn't do anything but go along for the ride, kiss her neck, and hope I could drop a double nut. Carmen rode me crazy for what felt like the next hour. Once we both came again, she moved off of me, went and grabbed a wash rag to clean me up, then she went and hopped in the shower. She took a quick shower while I stayed in bed and smoked a cigarette. After she got out, she climbed back in bed and had me rub lotion over her body while she sat between my legs; I as still pressed against the footboard. Once the lotion was properly applied, we stayed in that position essentially cuddling and talking for about twenty or thirty minutes, then I decided it was time to leave; it was pushing close to six in the morning and I'd been there for almost three hours.

I get up, put on my clothes and prepare to leave; Carmen gets partially dressed so that she can look outside and see if the coast's clear whenever I'm ready to leave. Before I leave, she gets me an extra toothbrush so I can brush my teeth and some gum. Once I feel good enough to leave, Carmen checks to see if anyone's in the hallway, particularly the CO NCO (charge of quarters noncommissioned officer) or the runner. The hall's empty, so we head to the exit and enter the stairwell. Once inside I let her know I was very appreciative of last night, or rather this morning, and we definitely had to do that again. She moved in closer, cheesing like a woman who'd been well pleased, and kisses me on the lips. We go at it in the stairwell, kissing passionately, and me grabbing her ass; she had no panties on, only a long T-shirt. We stop before things progress further or I'd never make it home. I give her one last peck on the lips and proceed to head down the stairs. She watched me as I left. Before I got to far down the stairs I stop, lean on the rails, look up at her and say," I thought you don't get wet for dudes, what happened in there?" She couldn't do nothing but smile, roll her eyes, and walk off. That's all I needed to hear, so I made my way to my truck.

Carmen and I fooled around a few more times over a six month period, but I cut her and several other women off after Lori and I got serious. As you can tell, things didn't exactly work out with the mother of my children, which is mainly my fault, but you live and you learn. If I hadn't met Lori I believe I could've locked Carmen up because she caught feelings and told me one night that she'd fallen in love with me after having some drinks and tooling around. Maybe it was the alcohol talking, but they say a drunken soul speaks a sober mind, or maybe she was dickmatized, who knows. Either way I enjoyed the experiences we had.

Janice

"I want to give you some love. I want to give you some good, good loving." Lauryn Hill and Bob Marley; *Turn the Lights Down Low*

I was a young, naive eighteen year old boy fresh out of high school, with no job and little money, when I received a phone call from a family friend about training me to drive tractor trailers. I had no plans at the time, so I said fuck it and moved in with him and his family. This arrangement worked out for about nine months, at which point I realized that this life wasn't for me. Plus, John and I didn't get along, so his wife Janice helped me get a job working with her as a prison guard.

Months passed and things were going pretty well until that one faithful day. On this day, my life changed after arriving home from work and conducting my normal routine of showering and later heading to the kitchen for something to drink. While going about my business, I noticed Janice standing in front of the mirror inspecting herself. I'm not a creep by far, but I couldn't help but stare at this mountain of a woman. Here was a sexy 30 year old, grown ass woman standing before me in a black lace bra that fought to contain her massive breasts. As I my eyes traveled down her body, my eyes landed on a perfectly round ass swallowing a matching pair of lace panties. I was mesmerized as I tried to process everything my young eyes took in on her short, thick, and compact frame. As I worked my way back up her body, I glimpsed an unforgettable butterfly tattoo wedged between those juicy tits. When I finally look up, we lock eyes in the mirror and she smiles at me, I think. Either way my trance was broken and I took me and my growing erection back to my room. I avoided her and the family for the rest of the night. All I could think of was the amazing features I'd witnessed and wondered if I'd have to fight her husband in the morning, however, nothing happened.

I continued working and following my normal routine, but something changed between us afterwards. By this, I mean we became more flirtatious and she dressed more provocative around the house. One Sunday afternoon, while drinking and talking about tattoos, she mentioned the butterfly between her succulent breasts. Me being me, I took this opportunity to ask what the entire tattoo looked like. Within seconds she's pulled open her blouse exposing the tattoo and a spillage of her big beautiful breasts. All I could think of at the time was 'Slim you got her now.' After that night, about two weeks later, John, Janice, and I were at a car dealership. Janice and I sat in the car waiting on John to come out when Lauryn Hill and Bob Marley's song *Turn the Lights Down Low* came on the radio. I was feeling myself, so I sang the chorus, "*I want to give you some love. I want to give you some good, good loving.*" Once I'm done, Janice boldly states,"*I hear you but you ain't trying to do nothing.*" I'm stunned and asked her to repeat what she said, to which she repeats herself loud and clear. I reply, *"Oh I* am!", and she tells me, *'We'll see."*

Roughly a month later, while John was locked up in weekend jail, a blizzard swept over the area. Janice asked me to go grocery shopping in case the weather got bad, so we get dressed and head out. I should've know something was up by the way she dressed. She wore skin tight Levi jeans with the red tab clenching for life around her juicy booty, a black silk shirt that hung off her exposed shoulders and her back, and some knee high boots over her jeans because they wouldn't fit underneath. Remember, A FUCKING BLIZZARD WAS GOING ON! Anyhow, she decided to go out of town instead of staying local, which again I found odd. While we shopped, I couldn't help but watch them cheeks send body shots to those jeans. I was captivated by her hypnotic sway and was caught looking several times, but was always greeted with a smile. We finished shopping, pay for our things, and exit the store to start our journey home. Some time before we arrive home I decide to go all out, so I asked her *"Whatsup? All this flirting and nothing ever happens."* Her answer catches me off guard when she exclaims, *"You dummy, why you think I dressed like this and had you drive to another state to get grocery in a blizzard?"* I think to myself 'you naive little nigga.' So I slam on brakes, almost slide into a ditch, and pop a U-turn to drive 30 minutes to a hotel, all the while not saying a word. Once I get there, I park the car, get a room, and take her inside.

Honestly, I was nervous as hell, because this woman was 10 years my senior and someone I'd crushed on since I was 15 and now I'm about to fuck; I'll explain the boyhood crush in Part Two. Anyhow, she gets settled while I head to the store. I purchased condoms and two drinks; why the drinks, I don't know, I told y'all I was nervous. When I got back to the room, she was in bed and her clothes on the floor. Now this wasn't my first time at the rodeo, however, this was a **:I year old WOMAN** with plenty of experience. So what do I do? I jet to the bathroom to get myself together, put on a condom, and get in the bed. I slid under the covers and felt the warmth radiating from her extravagant body. I looked into her eyes and thought that I was in over my head, but I'm Soldier Slim and I wasn't backing down.

We kiss and she grasps my arm and gently persuaded me into the missionary position. I entered her juicy pussy slowly and I notice one of the most amazing sites; her mouth opens and I hear her gasp. I immediately think 'Soldier Slim, we're in there now.' I massage her insides with slow, well placed strokes while she moans lightly in my ear and caressed my back. I know this isn't going to last much longer so I try to ease out slowly without drawing to much attention; however, she had other plans, so with a devilish grin she locks her legs around me keeping me in place. Within a couple of minutes I fill my condom full of hot seed, but I'd been waiting years for an opportunity like this, so I don't stop my stride. About 20 minutes later she rolls on top of me and starts riding me. I enjoyed the view of her tantalizing titties bouncing in my face and the way she controlled her position, and I knew it was only a matter of time, but I wasn't gonna cum twice before she did, that much I knew. So, I reached up and grabbed as much of her breasts as I could, smash her hard nipple together, and suckle on both. She immediately starts grinding harder and moaning louder, then places her hands behind my head causing her tits to press deeper in my mouth.

I feel like that got her, so I raise my pelvis up and strive to get as deep inside her as possible, still drinking from her well endowed breasts. It didn't take long for her to reach a climax as I felt her release with a grasp of my shaft. This caused me to lie back and she placed her hands on my chest and continued grinding as I explode for a second time. You'd think I'd be out for the count, but remember, I was still young, dumb, and full of cum. She slides off my dick and realizes that I'm still firm in nature. Janice reaches down and snatches off the useless, fully loaded condom and proceeds to place herself doggystyle, while pulling me behind her. With no questions asked I slide up in that hot, wet pussy going for a third round knockout. I watched her throw that ass back the way young girls claim they can, and I continue to work her from behind with some proper back shots. We reach our breaking point together and she asked me was I trying to give her a heart attack as I slide out of her pussy for what I assumed was the final time; I took that as a compliment and a TKO. We laid there for a while realizing that it was late, so we clean up, grabbed the two sodas, then drove home in silence. When we get home, I brought in the groceries. As I finished bring all the food in, I noticed her smoking on the back porch, so I man up once more and ask if it was a one time thing. She blew out the cigarette smoke, gave me that devilish grin, looked me right in my eyes and said, "No, this is only the beginning..."

Janice Pt. 2

John and Janice were people my family knew for along time. When I was 15 years old my father passed away and a couple of days later Janice picked me up from school and brought me a gold chain with a cross. Over twenty years later, I still remember that day. She wore tight black jeans and a low-cut African shirt that exposed her shoulders allowing an overflow of cleavage. I spent most of the day looking at the butterfly tattoo eye to eye, and in my head she allowed me to do so. A few months later my mother helped me purchase her some see-through nightgowns as a thank you gift. This may seem odd that I mentioned this, but it will come into play later.

Present Day: As Janice said, this was just the beginning. Our work schedule was chaotic, to say the least; I worked nights while she worked days, with alternating days off between us. So if her off days fell during the week they belonged to me. We initially decided not to fuck in the house, so she'd pick me up from work and we'd head to the Red Roof Inn. There was this one occasion where she was wore this little white sundress that barely, and I mean barely, covered her ass. I could see the bottom of her apple bottom booty bouncing all over the place as she lead me to the room. Seeing what I saw, and knowing what was about to transpire, I was at attention before we entered the room considering that this was technically the second time I was about to hit.

We get in the room and I know it's not going to be the last time so I'm ready to go, but she had different plans. I settle in, tum on the television, and she decides to tease me. She walked around the room bending over every so often so I could see her ass jiggle like Jell-0. I was laying on the bed as she slowly removed her dress, if you could call it that. She enticed me by sliding it slightly off her shoulder just below her breasts, she then turned around and let it fall below her tear drop ass, collecting on the floor. I'm in awe of the site standing before me in nothing but bra and panties; even though I knew she wasn't mine to possess, I felt like the luckiest guy EVER. Next, she climbed her fine self on top of me, and like Jay-Z said, she pulled her panties to the side and slide my rock hard dick inside her juicy goodness. She immediately starts moaning and grinding on me. I think she wanted this more than I did because not long after she cried out and came. Again I take this as a win, then I roll her ass over and continue to handle my business until I shoot her club up. Afterwards, we shower up and head home to pretend everything is normal.

I believe the song *"My Uttle Secret'* by Xscape reigned true, especially given the fact that we could all be in the same room and John not know I'm fucking his wife; that shit really turned me on, so you know I had to tum the heat up a little. One day after getting off and doing my usual, I noticed her yet again walking around the house, but this time she's wearing one of the gowns I'd bought years earlier. She kept passing by me, smiling, and I could see her nakedness underneath exposing those pretty brown nipples and ass cheeks bouncing around like a fun house with every step. So I go with the flow, walk up to her, and pin her between me and the wall. She plays coy and asked me what's going on, but I kiss her in response while holding her against the wall. I felt her nipples harden as I moved down her neckline. As I'm snacking on her neck she says nothing but *mmmhmm*. I continue to suck her neck as I free her breast from the restraint of her gown. At this point I'm hard enough to cut diamonds, and I'm pressing it against her. She acts ever the heroine and frees my erection from my pants and then rubs it. I continue to travel down her body, slowly unbuttoning the gown, sucking on her hardened nipples, and when I undo the last button there's nothing there but naked goodness. I slide a meaty finger inside her and massage her while she moans and groans in my ear. We do this dance for a while until she succumbs to the pressure I'm putting on her.

She grabs my hand and leads me to her bedroom. When we get there she fully frees me from my shorts and pushes me on the bed, then goes down to her knees placing me in her warm mouth. The entire time she's providing me fellatio her eyes are locked on me, watching my every expression. It seemed with every penetration of her jaws I wanted to release my juices down the back of her throat, but I withhold her that victory because I wanted what she had down south. I reached down, pulling her up, and remove the gown fully, then place her on all four. I ease my way inside her juicy center and try to knock her walls loose as I watch that ass bounce against my dick. The thing about it was the entire time this was happening, she was facing the mirror so I could see her titties bounce and it looked as it that butterfly tattoo was actually flying while her face registered pure joy. We go at it for a while, I'm gripping her hips and hitting her curves like I ain't have no breaks, long stroking her while holding her in place so she can't run, listening to her moan like a kitty on catnip. I feel her body tighten and relax and I know that she achieved another climax, so I know I can line her walls with my nut and finish up. After we're done, she grabs the blanket and sheets then runs butt naked to the washer. She comes back, grabs her gown, gives me a smile, and heads to the shower. We spend the rest of the day hanging out, talking, and chilling. Some time that evening, when it was time for everyone to come home, we put on our game faces and pretend everything is normal.

This game between us went on for months, there were even a couple of close calls where we almost got caught, but it ended up being tons of fun and I believe it was what we needed at that particular time in our lives. For me, it was a teenage fantasy come true and for her it was the thrill of a younger man allowing her to escape from normalcy. We knew it was wrong, but I wouldn't change it even if I could and I believe she wouldn't either.

Well, we hope you enjoyed Volume One of this series. We tried to keep it as raw and uncut as possible without being too vulgar. This was a glimpse into the lives of your servicemen and we welcome you for the journey in the near future. Who knows, some of you may even end up with a story of your own or an active participant! Here's a teaser from a Volume II story:

Camille

Give you a workout, have you burnin' calories. I'm tryna please you, just lay on yo back for me, then Imma need you to put on an act for me. It's just sum bout the way you look in lingerie. Girl. I can't letchu run away, girl you not Coi Leray.

- Feature by Lil Baby in *Addicted* with Chris Brown -

It was pushing midnight by the time Camille and I arrived at our Ranch style home. Camille's older sister, Candida, decided to keep the twin for the night so we could enjoy the rest of the night. I hit the garage button and park her BMW 745Li sitting on 22 inch Gianni's next to my decked out pearl white Denali truck on 24 inch Diablo's. Once we're inside I hit the button again to close the garage, kill the engine, and exit the driver side so that I could go open the door for my woman. As I opened the door, I took in the captivating beauty of my Black Queen: her expresso brown skin beat with a light coat of make-up; an obsidian and silver beaded necklace along with a silver chain carrying our family photo clutching her neck; her toned arms glistening in the light as I grasped her hand, her wrist showcasing several silver bangles.

As she exited the vehicle, I drink in the shape other exquisite body and the way her sleeveless black "freak em" dress envelops her body like an affection starved lover, with her and silver belt clutching her like interlocking arms. Her toned thighs are on full display as her dress found its way up her legs, revealing a meticulously clean shaven kitty; there was no need for her to be careful anymore as we were home. After catching a glimpse of her sweet African pie, I felt the blood rush from my brain to my manly region. Camille finally exited the car as both black heels connected with the cement floor, and her single braid tell in place right above her firm derriere; her Black and Native American bloodline was the cause for that.

She waits for me as I close the door, and take notice of how she matched her car with the black and silver thing going on. I reach out for her hand once the door is closed and I bring her close to me. I kiss her deeply, she moans as she pressed her naturally thick ass into her car and I press myself into her. Usually I'd have to bend a little to kiss my baby, but tonight-- with her six inch heels-- she easily stood 6'5" compared to my 6'8" frame. She was fully aware of my raging hard-on pressing against her, straining and jumping like an excited dog greeting its owner; I was ready to give it to her right there in the garage but thought better of it. After we finished kissing and dry hump, I breathlessly whisper in her ear, *"Happy Birthday once again baby, but I still have another gift before the night is over."*

To Be Continued in Volume Two

www.ingramcontent.com/pod-product-compliance
Lightning Source LLC
Chambersburg PA
CBHW070914100726
47907CB00008B/2321